Built to Last

Creation and Evolution:
A thoughtful look at the evidence that a
Master Designer created our planet

Dwight K. Nelson

Pacific Press® Publishing Association
Nampa, Idaho
Oshawa, Ontario, Canada

Edited by Harold G. Coffin and Kenneth R. Wade
Designed by Tim Larson
Cover illustration by Ron Lowery/The Stock Market©

Copyright © 1998 by
Pacific Press® Publishing Association
Printed in the United States of America
All Rights Reserved

ISBN 0-8163-1680-5

98 99 00 01 02 • 5 4 3 2 1

Contents

To Mom and Dad

"In the beginning . . ."

I'm grateful for scientists—these men and women who live out their days on the oftentimes unglamorous cutting edge of painstaking research and discovery. Not only have they made our world a better place, they keep teaching us more and more about this world they try to make better.

In this book that intersects the realm of science, I'm grateful to those scientists who have let me share in their lively dialogue for a time and who have broadened my perspectives and deepened my appreciation for science. The scientists who occupy what we call "the science complex" here at Andrews University have blessed me with their friendships. To all of them, thank you!

But in particular I'm thankful for a scientist living across the country in The Dalles, Oregon, who interrupted his retirement tranquillity to read and reread this manuscript—originally a series of sermons preached on this university campus at Pioneer Memorial Church. Dr. Harold Coffin—professsor, researcher, and author—brought the eye of a scientist and heart of a Christian scholar to these pages, and I'll always be grateful to him. His expertise in creation science was truly a godsend! Thank you!

Finally, a word of heartfelt gratitude for my first teachers in science and Creation, my parents, Barbara and Paul Nelson—who were with me "in the beginning." What I learned about God the Creator I learned first from them. For that alone, I am grateful and proudly indebted to my parents. Because of them this book is possible. For them this book is dedicated. With love on their fiftieth wedding anniversary.

Dwight K. Nelson
Pioneer Memorial Church Andrews University

Preface

Must science and religion be at war?

Are science and religion at war?

About a year after Charles Darwin published his seminal work, *The Origin of Species*, a debate was arranged between a minister and a scientist. Espousing the creationist point of view was Anglican Bishop Samuel Wilberforce. On the other side of the debate was Thomas Henry Huxley, a scientist and strong advocate of Darwin's evolutionary theory.

It was reported that the bishop—a good theologian but poor biologist (as related by Michael Behe in his book, *Darwin's Black Box*)—ended his speech by asking, "I beg to know, is it through his grandfather or grandmother that Huxley claims his descent from a monkey?"

Now, you don't have to be a seasoned debater to instantly assess that query as a very obvious low-blow kind of question! What opponent wouldn't become riled up with such a jab? The natural rejoinder would surely be a vehement, How dare you speak of my grandparents that way!

But that wasn't Huxley's retort. According to the story, he was overheard muttering with glee as he arose to the debate podium, "The Lord has delivered him into my hands!" (And that from an atheist scientist!)

Huxley then launched into a most erudite biology lesson for both the audience and the bishop. And at the end of his rebuttal, he declared that he did not know "whether it was through his grandmother or grandfather that he was related to an ape but that he would rather be descended from simians than be a man possessed of the gift of reason and see it used as the bishop had used it that day." Behe ends his telling of this story, "Ladies fainted, scientists cheered, and reporters ran to print the headline: 'War Between Science and Theology.' "[1]

But were they right? Are science and religion really at war? They don't need to be, do they? For are not science and religion both ever in quest of truth? Truth cannot contradict truth, can it? In fact, hasn't truth always borne up well under intense scrutiny? Of course.

It was Einstein who once said: "Religion without science is blind. Science without religion is lame." And years later John Polkinghorne came along—himself both an Anglican priest and physicist—and offered this refinement to Einstein: "I would say, 'Religion without science is confined; it fails to be completely open to reality. Science without religion is incomplete; it fails to attain the deepest possible understanding.' "[2] They must go together.

After all, both realms of knowledge are faced with the identical question of origins: Where did we come from; how did we get here? While the answers and the methodologies for finding them are not always the same, the quest and question are. Where did we come from; how did we get here? Stephen Hawking, the great English astrophysicist, framed that most basic of all questions with this bit of musing: "Why does the universe go to all the bother of existing?"[3]

This book is being written in quest of that answer. And in searching for the answer, we will not be looking merely for information to settle a debate. The issue at hand is, Where did we come from, and where are we going? Are we as humans just the product of some evolutionary accident, and will our final end be just as accidental? Or were we designed by a Creator, who has an eternal plan for us? Were we built just for one lifetime, or were we built to last for eternity?

Right here "in the beginning," here at the outset, I feel compelled to declare a list of caveats before this journey has even begun! Call them apologies or disclaimers, if you will. I don't mind. They must be expressed here.

Caveat number one: It almost goes without saying (but I must declare it anyway) that there are much brighter minds than mine that are wrestling over the great issues and questions that science and religion interface. By taking on the debate between creation and evolution, I am in no way suggesting that I have become an authority in either realm!

I have the privilege of pastoring at Andrews University, and in this parish I am surrounded by bright and intelligent minds, both scientific and theological, that are steeped in the disciplines that inform the journey this book is undertaking. I am grateful for these men and women who are highly respected within and outside my community of faith. Once a quarter I have the privilege of joining a group of them for a luncheon discussion of yet another issue over which science and religion wrestle. I enjoy sharing their dialogue and probing their thinking. I thank God for gifted specialists in all disciplines. We need them all.

My point? While I have endeavored to read widely and carefully in preparation for this journey, that in no way confers the status of specialist or authority upon me. Greater minds than mine (and perhaps even yours) are wrestling with the great issues of origin.

Caveat number two: In the matter of human origins, there are some significant conundrums and puzzles and questions and discoveries that are very difficult to answer. Proponents of both sides of the creation versus evolution debate recognize that there simply is not an airtight case in favor of one over the other. It would be foolish to undertake a book like this and not candidly note at the outset that all the questions have *not* been answered and all the riddles have *not* been solved. If this were an airtight case, we would all be singing off the same page of the hymnal. And yes, it would be a hymnal! But it is not, and we are not.

Caveat number three: There are obvious limitations to any treatment of the creation versus evolution debate. Dusty tomes, ponderous books, and scholarly journals dealing with the subject of our concern fill shelves upon shelves in libraries. I am fully aware that the eight chapters that follow in this volume cannot possibly treat the issues comprehensively.

Why then do I undertake to write this book? Actually, I did not set out to write one. During the winter of 1997 I preached a series of sermons in the Pioneer Memorial Church, on the campus of Andrews University, addressing the faith challenge that the contemporary Christian faces in a secular society seemingly bent on expunging God from its philosophy of life. How can Christians, like the three thousand students and the two hundred faculty on this campus, be both intellectual and faithful in the face of the mounting Darwinian challenge? How can we fulfill the biblical admonition: "Always be ready to make your defense to anyone who demands from you an accounting for the hope that is in you"? (1 Pet. 3:15).[4] In response to those questions, I wrote and preached a series of sermons. These have been modified and appear as the eight chapters that follow.

I must also testify that the further I delved into the creation/evolution debate and the further the congrega-

tion and I went through the series, the firmer grew my
pastoral conviction that a contemporary faith in the biblical accounts of the Creator and Creation can indeed intelligently withstand the frontal assault of Darwin's
theory. In fact, I was astounded to learn along the way
that there is fresh, new information being discovered by
science, stunning knowledge that powerfully defends and
supports the biblical teaching of creation "in the beginning." The believer, young or aged, educated or illiter-
ate, can offer an articulate, logical, and informed "reason
for the hope that is within." And all of it without apol-
ogy. It was that conclusion at the end of the sermon series that led me to write this pastoral perspective in the
debate over human origins.

The fourth and final caveat: No matter what conclusions you and I may come to, whether in agreement or
disagreement, there is no place in the community of Christ
for the spirit of arrogance or intolerance. Yes, there is
truth. And we must defend that truth! But none of us can
garner a monopoly of truth and knowledge over all others. We need each other, and we must keep talking and
listening to one another.

Yes, there is a risk, but legal scholar Phillip Johnson
absolutely is right in his book, *Reason in the Balance*:

> To enter the field of intellectual argument is
> to accept the risk that we may lose by being proved
> wrong. But accepting the risk of being wrong is
> the inescapable price for making any meaningful
> statements about the world. The best scientists
> have never feared to accept the risk—which is why
> they have learned so much and also why they have
> placed themselves at risk by overextending their
> territory. Those who will not take a risk end up

saying nothing at all, like a violinist who stops
playing for fear of hitting a wrong note.[5]

It is risky dealing with this subject from the pulpit or
in a book. At the beginning of our congregational journey, people came to me, whistled through their teeth, and
wished me good luck (with the implication that fools rush
in where angels fear to tread!). But actually, we are not
in need of good luck. We need God's light.

His truth can bear examination—prayerful, careful
examination. So with a prayer for one another, I invite
you to join me in the journey; a journey that won't end
with the last page of this book; a journey whose ending
is promised "in the beginning" with God.

Dwight K. Nelson
Fall 1997
Pioneer Memorial Church
Andrews University

1. Michael J. Behe, *Darwin's Black Box* (New York: The Free Press, 1996),
236.

2. John Polkinghorne, *Serious Talk: Science and Religion in Dialogue* (Val-
ley Forge: Trinity Press International, 1995), 75.

3. Kitty Ferguson, *The Fire in the Equations: Science, Religion, and the
Search for God* (Grand Rapids: William B. Eerdmans Publishing Company, 1994), 6.

4. Unless otherwise indicated, all scripture references are from the New
Revised Standard Version of the Bible.

5. Phillip E. Johnson, *Reason in the Balance: The Case Against Naturalism in Science, Law and Education* (Downers Grove: InterVarsity Press,
1995), 109, 110.

CHAPTER ONE

Fatal Attraction

Writing at the end of the year in the *London Times* Literary Supplement, Galen Strawson bemoaned how hard this millennium has been on "human hubris," our pride as a species. After all, look what the last few centuries have brought us:

> Copernicus displaced us from the centre of the universe, Darwin closed Eden, showing that we are apes with shrews for ancestors and cabbages for cousins. Freud pointed out that we are not our own masters even in our own heads. . . . [And] modern genetics showed that we share over 98 per cent of our genes with chimpanzees.[1]

Strawson's unsubtle point? Thanks to Copernicus, Darwin, Freud, and modern genetics, we as humans have been whittled down to size. And way down, at that! We may have thought once upon a time we were a race of special somebodies. But not any longer. Because when "Darwin closed Eden," Strawson pines, we learned the truth that "we are apes with shrews for ancestors and cabbages for cousins." With a family tree like that, who could blame us for feeling blue!

But I'd like to ask Strawson some questions of my own: Are we humans then condemned to live out our days in that blue funk haze of accidental insignificance? Must we allow Darwin and Freud and Copernicus to convince us that we have no destiny or design? Are mere humans able to destroy our belief in Creation?

In search of the answers, we must begin "in the beginning" with an *a priori*. In case you're not familiar with it, *a priori* is an old Latin phrase meaning "from what is before," and when it's used today, it refers to the presuppositions we all use every day. In fact, it's impossible not to have *a prioris*.

For example, when you study the American Declaration of Independence, you presuppose that its principal author, Thomas Jefferson, really did exist. You never met him in your lifetime, nor have you met anybody who has met him. But you've read about him, and you've read documents that have been passed down through the generations that claim to prove that he was the author of the Declaration of Independence. You have even read the testimony of people who knew him centuries ago. And so you accept, as an *a priori*, that Thomas Jefferson really did exist and in fact did write the document you're about to study.

You have to accept this *a priori* by faith, because you have no way to personally prove that Thomas Jefferson wrote the Declaration of Independence or even that he existed.

You make another *a priori* assumption every time you deposit money in a bank. You accept, by faith, that the bank will actually deposit your money and that it will be there when you need to withdraw it. You ask for no proof, except your deposit slip. You simply accept the *a priori* "truth" that banks are reliable institutions.

We live in a world where *a prioris* reign in abundance.

Not surprisingly then, our journey into the heart of the debate between creation and evolution is laden with *a prioris* too. In the chapters that follow we will carefully examine the *a priori* premises that undergird Darwin's evolutionary theory. But first consider the fact that the Holy Scriptures operate with a very critical *a priori* too. In fact, there are three of them in Hebrews 11:

A priori *one:* "Whoever would approach him [God] must believe that he exists" (Hebrews 11:6). Clearly the Scriptures are predicated upon the premise or presupposition that there is a God. God exists!

The great philosopher Pascal masterfully dealt with this *a priori* in his famed analogy of "The Wager":

> This much is certain, either God is, or He is not; there is no middle ground. But to which view shall we be inclined? Think of a coin being spun which will come down either heads or tails. How will you wager? Reason can't make you choose either, reason can't prove either wrong in advance. . . . But you *must* wager, for you are already committed to life, and not to wager that God is, is to wager that He is not. Which side, then, do you take?
>
> Let's weigh the gain or loss involved in calling heads that God exists: If you win, you win everything, if you lose, you lose nothing. Don't hesitate then; wager that He does exist. For there is an infinity of infinitely happy life to be won, and what you're staking is finite. That leaves no choice. Since you are obliged to play, you must

be renouncing reason if you hoard your life rather than risk it for an infinite gain which is just as likely to occur as a loss amounting to nothing.[2]

Of course, the Bible is a passionate appeal to the reader to "make the wager" of faith that indeed God exists. That He does is the first of three critical *a prioris* in the Bible.

A priori *two:* "Whoever would approach him [God] must believe that he exists and that he rewards those who seek him" (Heb. 11:6). The Scriptures call us to add to the fact of God's existence the *a priori* premise that He is a personal Being who invites us to seek Him and who will reward us when we do. He is not some distant Landlord. He is Someone who longs for personal companionship with us. And when we seek Him, this *a priori* declares, He rewards our quest. And that reward is His reciprocal revealing of Himself to our seeking minds. What a God! But there is a third *a priori* the Bible invites us to embrace.

A priori *three:* "By faith we understand that the worlds were prepared by the word of God, so that what is seen was made from things that are not visible" (Heb. 11:3). The Scriptures include a third premise for us as we start our faith journey; namely, "we understand that the worlds were prepared by the word of God." This personal Being who exists as God and who rewards all those who seek Him is the same One who created the worlds! The Greek literally reads that "the ages" were created by God's word. The *New International Version* translates this line, "By faith we understand that the universe was formed at God's command." By His word He created the entire universe! That *a priori* is presupposed from Genesis through to Revelation.

So there they are—plain and simple, yet profound and

deep—three faith *a prioris* critical for any quest for truth within the covers of the Holy Scriptures. All three premises are introduced by the opening verse of Hebrews 11: "Now faith is the assurance of things hoped for, the conviction of things not seen." The Greek word for "conviction" or "evidence" in this verse can also be translated as "proof." Which means that faith is "the proof of things not seen."

But how can faith "prove" anything? It does all the time, actually. Most of us have never seen the generator that produces the electricity that fires up the light bulbs, televisions, hair dryers, and CD players in our homes. And yet every time we switch on one of our appliances, we surround ourselves with 120 volts of shocking proof that somewhere there is an unseen generator that in fact does exist. I'd feel rather foolish trying to argue against the existence of that unseen generator, surrounded as I am by proofs of its reality!

Even so, Hebrews 11, the great Hall of Faith and Fame chapter of the Bible, opens with the resounding declaration that human faith believes that what it observes all around it is ample evidence (evidentiary proof, if you please) for the truth of the three great *a prioris*—God exists, He is a personal Being who rewards those who seek Him, and He is the One who created the universe. You can't prove those *a prioris* true any more than you can prove the existence of Thomas Jefferson. But faith accepts their veracity, just as it accepts Jefferson's historicity.

But some people don't want to have to take any *a prioris* by faith—they choose to believe it when they see it. This, of course, is a ridiculous position to maintain and defend! There isn't a credible scientist around who won't admit that science itself is dependent on *a priori* faith. Only they don't call it faith–they refer to it as "spectacles behind the eyes" or "filters through which they view the world"—these premises and presuppositions that scientists accept without any proof at all. Listen to Kitty Ferguson, graduate of Julliard School of Music, turned science writer from Cambridge University, in her book *The Fire in the Equations*:

> The assumtions underlying the scientific method are not capable of being proved of disproved by the scientific method. If [Kurt] Godel was right [a German mathematician who came up with the theorem now known as Godel's Incompleteness Theorem, which proved that there are propositions that can be stated in mathematical whole number systems but cannot be proved], belief in mathematics also requires a leap of faith. . . . Even in mathematics, truth goes beyond our ability to prove that it is true. One definition of religion has it that a religion is a system of thought which requires one to believe in "truths" which can't be proved. If that's what a religion is, then according to Godel's Theorem, mathematics is a religion. In fact, mathematician F. De Sua has remarked that it seems to be the only religion that has proved it *is* a religion.[3]

Mark it down, and mark it well—both science and religion are dependent upon faith *a prioris*. Beware of the one who criticizes your faith by claiming that such "leaps" belong only to religion! He doesn't know what he is talking about! So, if "seeing is believing" is your methodology for life, then you are operating on an impossible fantasy. Because we are irrevocably finite (as humans we have a beginning and we will have an end) we cannot go everywhere and see everything ourselves, we have no choice but to accept in science and religion some things by faith. Life is too short to prove everything.

What, then, shall we conclude from all this? We all have to start somewhere—scientists, religionists, atheists, agnostics, and believers alike—none of us comes to this journey with what the Latins called a *tabula rasa*—a clean slate. It is ludicrous to believe otherwise. Already there is writing on the slates of our minds as we begin to consider the issue of creation versus evolution. For Christians the writing on the slate is the *a priori* of the Holy Scriptures. Christian faith in its simplest and in its most complex forms embraces the existence of an eternal Creator God through whom all life exists. And, Christian faith in its most fundamental expression—and I use that term advisedly—also embraces the *validity* of the biblical accounts of Creation and the *veracity* of the Creation story. We begin with the understanding that the Bible is true.

The old farmer testified, "If God said it, I believe it." Does such a confession belong only on a bumper sticker?

I realize that many people believe that there is no such thing as objective truth—but I am indebted to Philip Johnson who retorts, "To insist that there is no such thing as objective truth is to state a purportedly objective truth, and this is self-contradictory."[4]

We are all in search of truth. But we ought not to be too quick in dismissing the old farmer's confession—"If God said it, I believe it."

What did God say about Creation and origins?

"Oh, but come on, Pastor," you might respond. "God didn't say that. The words of Scripture were certainly not dictated by God—we all know that. Moses (or whoever wrote Genesis) was the one who told the story of

Creation. God may have inspired some thoughts, but the man came up with the story. You can't take it literally!"

If that is your thinking I respond, "Oh, he did? Did he come up with the story himself to illustrate some great idea or thought—is that it?" What did the farmer confess? "If God said it, I believe it." OK, then, let's take your hypothesis and let the Creation story be one man's reflections on some inspired thoughts. But what shall we do with the fourth commandment? "Remember the Sabbath day, and keep it holy. . . . For in six days the Lord made heaven and earth, the sea, and all that is in them" (Exod. 20:8, 11). What shall we do with the fourth commandment? After all, was it not written by the finger of God on a table of stone? "Oh, but come now, Pastor— you don't really believe that one, do you? Come on! You can't take it literally!"

You see what is happening, my friend? Can you see? As soon as you abandon the old farmer's adage, "If God said it, I believe it," you are headed down a dangerous road. Watch where it leads:

"He didn't create the world in the way the first chapters of Genesis purports"—that was a symbolic myth given merely to illustrate God's power. You can't take it literally!

Once you accept that idea, it's not far to the next, and each step leads to another:

"He didn't write the six-day Creation account with His own finger on stone"—that was literary hyperbole to elevate those ten laws for the sake of the generations that would follow. You can't take it literally!

"He didn't create male and female in one day from the dust of the ground and from Adam's rib"—that was only a simplified version of evolutionary development and reflected the male chauvinism of the times. You can't take it literally!

"She didn't give birth as a virgin to her son"—that's impossible. That was merely an earnest and sincere attempt by the early Christian community to declare that her son was indeed a special person and a great leader. You can't take it literally!

"He didn't go through the villages giving miraculous healing to all who were sick"—those accounts were not written down until oral retelling through the years had brought in much corruption and exaggeration. You can't take it literally!

"And He didn't rise from the dead and the grave"—that simply cannot be done. The resurrection story was carefully invented to symbolize that the life philosophy of the executed and dead Jesus of Nazareth could bring the rebirth of new hope and courage to the downtrodden and the despairing masses they were attempting to reach. You can't take it literally!

See what happens once you start out to question the validity of any part of the Bible? Where do we stop? When does human reason yield to faith as the court of final appeal? And who decides? The scientists? The philosophers? The theologians? The pope?

In Pope John Paul II's message to the Pontifical Academy of Sciences on October 22, 1996, which was convened to discuss the origins of life, are a number of statements that accept evolution as a reasonable explanation for human origin. Note his words:

> In his encyclical *Humani Generis* (1950), my predecessor Pius XII had already stated that there was no opposition between evolution and the doctrine of the faith about man and his vocation, on condition that one did not lose sight of several in-

disputable points. . . .

Today, almost half a century after the publica-
tion of the encyclical, new knowledge has led to
the recognition of more than one hypothesis in the
theory of evolution. It is indeed remarkable that
this theory has been progressively accepted by researchers following a series of discoveries in various fields of knowledge. The convergence, neither sought nor fabricated, of the results of work
that was conducted independently is in itself a significant argument in favor of this theory.[5]

Let the human organism evolve from preexisting living matter, the pope tells the academy—in fact earlier in
the text he stated that "there was no opposition between
evolution and the doctrine of the faith about man"—just
make sure you remember that God put the spiritual soul
into that evolved body. He emphasizes a declaration made
by a previous pope. "Pius XII stressed this essential point:
If the human body takes its origin from pre-existent living matter, the spiritual soul is immediately created by
God." And so Rome announces to the world of science,
you can bring your theory and be at home here. Evolution gave us the physical body, but God supernaturally
created the spiritual soul.

But wait a minute. How can you accept the idea that
humans evolved from lower life forms without abandon-
ing the Bible's account of Creation?

You can't logically defend such a position. Because
if you abandon belief in Creation on the basis of logic
and science how can you continue to believe in the virgin birth and resurrection of the Son of God? From a
logical standpoint, all miracles must stand or fall together.

You see, the quest for accommodation and acceptance

has always been a fatal attraction. Attractive? Yes. We all sense the tug to accommodate in order to be accepted. But fatal. For severed from the Holy Scriptures, faith always dies.

1. *Newsweek*, 30 December 1996; 6 January 1997, 136.

2. Blaise Pascal, *Pensees*, no. 418, in Howard A. Peth, *Seven Mysteries . . . Solved!* vol. 1 (La Puente, Calif.: Lessons From Heaven, Inc., 1988), 15.

3. Kitty Ferguson, *The Fire in the Equations: Science, Religion and the Search for God* (Grand Rapids: William B. Eerdmans Pub. Co., 1994), 6.

4. Philip Johnson, *Reason in the Balance: The Case Against Naturalism in Science, Law and Education* (Downer's Grove: InterVarsity Press, 1995), 116.

5. John Paul II, "Message to Pontifical Academy of Sciences on Evolution" in *Origins*, 1996. pp. 350-352.

CHAPTER TWO

The Achilles' Heel of the Java Man

On the ceiling of the Sistine Chapel in the Vatican is one of the great masterpieces of human creativity and art in Michelangelo's renowned painting, *The Creation of Adam*. I suppose God's and Adam's fingers nearly touching tip to tip, as portrayed in this painting, are the two most famous fingertips in all of history. As one art critic described it: "Michelangelo uses God and man as protagonists and infuses each with qualities of the other to achieve a physical impact with sublime overtones rarely if ever matched?"[1] It is truly a classic depiction of that creation moment.

This painting gives a high view of man reaching out, reaching up to his Creator. The theory of evolution takes an opposite view. Rather than crediting a higher being with our creation, evolutionists would ask us to look to lower forms of life for our origin.

Did humans descend from apes or monkeys?

Someone sent me the following humorous poem that looks at this question from another angle.

Three Monkeys

Three monkeys sat on a coconut tree
Discussing things that are said to be.
Said one to the others, "Now listen, you two,
There's a terrible rumor that can't be true
That man descended from our great race,—
Why, brother, the idea's an awful disgrace.

A monkey never beat his wife,
Harmed her children and ruined her life.
And other things you'll never see
Is an ape who's drunk and out on a spree,
Wielding a gun or club or knife
To take some other monkey's life . . .

Yes, man descended,—the ornery cuss—
But brother, he never descended from us."[2]

If we didn't descend from monkeys, how did we get here? That question is at the heart of the raging controversy between Darwinism and theism—between the theory that all life evolved from an ancient spark of life through evolution and the theory that all life has come from the hands of a benevolent Creator God. In short, are we descended from apes, or were we created by God?

Evolutionists may not appreciate the over-simplification that phrasing the debate in such terms may suggest. And the fact is, some of them believe in a Creator who originated life but allowed the process of evolution to bring development to the present state. I believe that it is important for Christians to respect the sincerity that many evolutionists demonstrate. There is nothing to be gained by trivializing or ridiculing their sincere attempts to understand where we have come from. Certainly, the golden rule is applicable in this heated debate—treat others the way you yourself want to be treated—with courtesy and respect.

This does not mean that Christian thinkers should not vigorously challenge every *a priori*, every premise, every presupposition, and carefully examine every piece of evidence that evolutionists proffer to support their theory. And so we move straight to the heart of the evolutionary debate by challenging the fossil record (or lack thereof) that evolutionists depend on to prove that humans have evolved from lower apelike forms.

Before turning to the fossils, let's consider again the majestic cadence of the Holy Scriptures' grand prologue: **In the beginning God created the heaven and the earth (Gen. 1:1, KJV).**

These are some of the most familiar words in all the Holy Writ, known well by atheists, agnostics, and believers alike. The words of Genesis 1:1 were quoted without comment by an American astronaut who, peering out of his space capsule portal upon the white-laced, blue-green terrestrial ball, as seen from orbit around the moon, repeated these words verbatim to Mission Control in Houston. These same words, shaped into metal letters, are embedded in stone around the plaza of the science complex at Andrews University where I work, a daily visual reminder of the *a priori* premise and presupposition that guides the Christian scientist in her research and in his teaching.

Bereshith bara Elohim—that is how the Hebrew begins. *Bereshith*, the Book of Beginnings, "In the beginning." The Greeks translated this Hebrew book into their own language and chose the word for "generations" *(geneseo)* in chapter 2:4, thus calling the book Genesis, from whence comes our English title. In every language the opening salvo of this ancient Writ is the same, "In the beginning God created the heaven and the earth"—*Bereshith bara Elohim.*

> . . . the earth was a formless void and darkness covered the face of the deep, while a wind from God swept over the face of the waters. Then God said, "Let there be light"; and there was light. And God saw that the light was good; and God separated the light from the darkness. God called the light Day, and the darkness he called Night. And there was evening and there was morning, the first day (Gen. 1:2-5).

Five days later, according to this account, came the creation of the human race.

Then God said, "Let us make humankind in our image, according to our likeness; and let them have dominion over the fish of the sea, and over the birds of the air, and over the cattle, and over all the wild animals of the earth, and over every creeping thing that creeps upon the earth."

> So God created humankind in his
> image,
> in the image of God he created
> them;
> male and female he created them (Gen. 1:26, 27).

Having read the ancient creation account, let us turn now to what I like to call "The Achilles' Heel of the Java Man." You've probably heard of Java Man, Peking Man, and Nebraska Man. These are all reconstructed "pre-human humans" that you often see in museums, encyclopedias, and textbooks. These depictions are based on evolutionists' ideas of our origins.

In reality, the Java Man had no Achilles' heel at least it's never been found! In fact, the pictures you see of Java Man are based on just five body parts (three teeth, one leg bone, and part of a skull) discovered by a Dutch army physician named Eugene Dubois. In 1891 Dr. Dubois traveled to the Solo River near the village of Trinil, Java, in Indonesia, for the announced purpose of discovering primitive man! He first found the skull cap along the bank of a river. About a year later he found two molar teeth and a human femur fifteen meters away from the skull cap. In 1898 he discovered a premolar tooth that he believed also belonged to his first find. Despite the fact that they were widely scattered, Dubois concluded that they belonged together. From these five fragments, he constructed what he later called *Pithecanthropus erectus* (Greek, erect ape-man), popularly known as the Java Man. Evolutionists have concluded that this represents an early precursor to humankind that lived about a half million years ago.

Pictures and reconstructions of the Java Man began to appear in museums, giving "the unsuspecting public the impression that the specimen must have been quite intact."[3] But the entire reconstruction was based on five fragments found scattered in sediments deposited on the river bank. Dubois triumphantly declared that his find "represents a so-called transition form between man and apes . . . the immediate progenitor of the human race."[4]

Because the scientific community for the most part did not accept his conclusions, Dubois kept his fossils out of sight of scientists for thirty years. He also kept secret during that time the fact that he had found two human skulls (now known as the Wadjak skulls) not far away and at approximately the same level of excavation.

Why did he keep this quiet? Because knowledge of their discovery would have weakened his assertion that the five bones he first found belonged to some intermediate form of life between man and ape. He did not wish to deal with contrary evidence—a problem that has arisen more than once in the study of ancient human remains. Earnest Albert Hooton, an evolutionary anthropologist from Harvard University, has written, "Heretical and nonconforming fossil men [have been] banished to the limbo of dark museum cupboards, forgotten or even destroyed."[5] In other words, Dubois was not the only one to hide or ignore evidence that didn't fit the conclusions he wanted to draw.

Before he died, Dubois changed his mind and declared that the "erect ape-man" he had discovered closely resembled a large gibbonlike ape. Ironically, by that time most of the scientific community had bought into his first assertions, accepting the idea that his Java Man was one of the missing links in evolution that they had been looking for.

Another case with some similarity was that of Nebraska Man, "discovered" in 1922 by Harold Cook and based on only a single tooth. Cook mailed the tooth to the famous paleontologist (fossil specialist) Henry Fairfield Osborn, director of the American Museum of Natural History in New York City. Osborn was fascinated by the find and compared it with all the descriptions, casts, and drawings he could find then consulted three other scientists, two of whom were eminent specialists on fossil primates. After much deliberation, they announced that here was proof of early man on the North American continent and published their discovery in the journal *American Museum Novitates* as follows:

It is hard to believe that a single water-worn tooth . . . can signalize the arrival of the anthropoid primates in North America. . . . We have been eagerly anticipating some discovery of this kind, but were not prepared for such convincing evidence. . . !⁶

Osborn and his colleagues couldn't quite decide whether the original owner of this tooth should be classed an apelike man or a manlike ape. He was given the distinguished scientific name *Hesperopithecus haroldcookii* ("Harold Cook's Western Ape"). The London *Daily Illustrated News* displayed a full-page spread on Nebraska Man, reconstructing his exact shape, even to the prominent brow ridges and broad shoulders—from a single tooth!

But, alas, two years later Nebraska Man's career, as Peth puts it, came to an abrupt halt! It turns out he was not a man; he was not even an ape. The tooth proved later to be that of a fossil *peccary*, which is a wild animal related to the domestic pig. Gish later wrote, "I believe this is a case in which a scientist made a man out of a pig and the pig made a monkey out of the scientist."⁷

Why do I share this with you? To make fun of evolutionists? Not at all! Remember the golden rule. It is imperative, however, that we share information like this in order to reveal the lack of fossil evidence to support the belief that humans evolved from some apelike ancestor.

There are fossilized skeletons that, if approached by evolutionary presuppositions, could be construed to resemble some sort of half-man, half-ape. What follows are the most commonly used examples of human evolution.⁸

RAMAPITHECUS—Teeth and parts of a jaw that were found in India in 1932 were thought to be a fossil hominid (some subhuman creature in line to become human later through evolutionary development). However, further studies now link those fossils to chimpanzees or baboons that are still living in Africa.

AUSTRALOPITHECUS—Fossils of this type were first discovered in South Africa by Dart in 1924 and Leakey in Tanzania in 1959. Further study of all available fragments of these skeletons by two eminent British scientists, Zuckerman and Oxnard, indicates that the animals represented did not resemble either man, chimpanzee, or gorilla but constituted a category of their own.[9] However, if we saw one alive today, we probably would not hesitate to call it an ape.

Donald Johanson's "Lucy" (an australopithecine) was discovered in 1973 in Ethiopia. Based on remains equaling 40 percent of the total skeleton, the individual (a female) was calculated to be a little over a meter tall and having about one-third the brain capacity of modern humans. She was claimed to be a bipedal (walking on two feet) hominid three and one-half million years old. Remains of several more individuals have subsequently been found. Further study of all this material has dimmed the opinion that "Lucy" was truly bipedal and the hope that she could become the true "missing link."

HOMO HABILIS—First discovered by Leakey's son Richard and called Skull 1470, it was considered to be intermediate between *Australopithecus* and *Homo erectus* (Java Man). The recent discovery of parts of the skeleton has shown this specimen to be more apelike than formerly thought. There is some concern that *Homo habilis* may be a mosaic constructed from pieces of more than one species.

NEANDERTHAL MAN—Illustrations showed him to be a primitive brutelike human for many years until it became evident that he was fully human, although perhaps from a race different from any alive today. The skeleton on which the original descriptions were based probably was deformed by disease. His cranial capacity was equal to or greater than that of modern humans.

CRO-MAGNON MAN was almost a superman. His beautiful artistry can be seen in caves in southern France and northern Spain. Neither Neanderthal nor Cro-Magnon can be used as evidence of our evolution from apes.

A number of other ancient human remains have been found, but they are either questionable, fragmentary, or of no significance for human evolution. PILTDOWN MAN occupied an important position on the evolutionary family tree for many years until it was discovered that someone had pieced together part fossil, part fresh bone, part ape, and part human remains to construct a skull. Considering the obvious traces of fraud, how could so many researchers be fooled for so long? This episode is a commentary on the blinders a strong bias can place on the eyes of even scientists!

Yes, some of these ancient men lived in caves, but that is hardly proof of subhumans or primitive existence. People still live in caves today. In fact, when I was discussing the weakness of the caveman argument with my wife and daughter one evening at supper, Kristin piped up with "Cavemen are human beings, Daddy. After all, Doug Batchelor lived in a cave, didn't he?"[10] She does have a point!

There they are—the great fossil evidences that keep falling dreadfully short of Darwin's premise that somewhere, someday, the "missing link" between the human and the ape will be found in the fossil record. We have been told that there is an abundance of evidence!

What then is the Achilles' heel of the Java Man, when in fact he had no Achilles' heel? Ah, it is the Achilles' heel of every single one of the supposed transitional fossil skeletons between man and ape we just noted: *There simply is no reliable fossil proof that a transitional life-form between the ape and the human ever existed on this earth.* I repeat, no convincing fossil evidence has yet been found to prove Darwin's hypothesis that humans evolved from apes or apelike creatures.

Where, then, did we all come from? Where shall we turn for the answer? The words of Genesis 1:26, 27 are clear. But just in case you are still not ready to embrace the creation accounts of Genesis, let us look elsewhere in Scripture. You are not ready yet to embrace the old farmer's confession we noted in the first chapter, "If God said it, I believe it." As a Christian, would you be willing to make this testimony? "If Jesus said it, I believe it?"

Let's consider what Jesus had to say on this subject.

Some Pharisees came to him, and to test him they asked, "Is it lawful for a man to divorce his wife for any cause?" He answered, "Have you not read that the one who made them at the beginning 'made them male and female,' and said, 'for this reason a man shall leave his father and mother and be joined to his wife, and the two shall become one flesh'? So they are no longer two, but one flesh. Therefore what God has joined together, let no one separate" (Matt. 19:3-6).

Note that in the above statement Jesus quoted directly from Genesis 1:27 and 2:24. He asked the scholars, "Have you not read?" Read what? Haven't you read the book of Genesis? Haven't you read the Creation story? Don't you believe what you read there? That God created the human race out of one male and one female? In the Gospel of Mark's telling of the story, Jesus declares, "From the beginning of Creation" humans have existed (Mark 10:6). In essence, Jesus says "You know the story of Creation—you accept the authority as I do of the Genesis accounts—how does the record read?"

There is no question concerning Creation if you accept the gospel teachings of Christ as recorded in Matthew and Mark. If you don't accept them, then the scriptural witness means nothing to you anyway and you have no choice but to accept the fossil record in spite of how scarce its evidence is. But if you do accept the Gospel accounts, then there is no question that Jesus accepted the Genesis accounts of Creation as true. Period. And if Jesus said it, then I believe it.

Am I being too naive? I think not! And were we to pose the question to Him, "Lord Jesus, did we evolve from lower life forms and primates?" what do you suppose He would answer? Surely His answer would be the same! "Have you not read that from the beginning of creation, God made them male and female? Haven't you read the book of Genesis?" I ask you, Why should He answer us any differently today than He did the scholars of His time?

Perhaps this same Jesus would also conclude His answer to us the same way He did with those scholars: "What God has joined together, let no one separate." Don't let anyone separate you from the Creation story, because any teaching or philosophy or theory that would separate us from the Genesis account of Creation will in the end separate us from the very Jesus who taught the Creation story "in the beginning." Was He a fool for believing that account? Or was He telling us the truth? You can't have it both ways. The question of what you believe about Creation finally comes down to a question of what you believe about Jesus.

As for me, if He said it, I believe it!

---

1. Joseph Satin, *The Humanities Handbook* (New York: Holt Rinehart & Winston, Inc.: 1969), 192.

2. Author unknown, brought to my attention by my friend Ed Higgins.

3. Eugene Dubois in Howard A Peth, *Seven Mysteries . . . Solved!* (La Puente, Calif.: Lessons from Heaven, Inc., 1988), 1:149.

4. Peth, 149.

5. Earnest A. Hooton in Peth, 1:151.

6. Henry F. Osborn in Peth, 1:155.

7. Duane T. Gish, *Evolution: The Fossils Say No* (San Diego: Creation-Life Publishers, 1979), 130.

8. Colin Mitchell, *The Case for Creationism* (Alma Park, England: Autumn House Ltd., 1994).

9. Charles E. Oxnard, *Fossils, Teeth and Sex, a New Perspective on Human Evolution* (Seattle: University of Washington Press, 1987), 227.

10. Pastor Doug Batchelor had recently conducted a series of meetings in the area. In his youth, previous to his conversion, he had lived for a time in a cave.

CHAPTER THREE

Darwin's Black Box

Is it possible that something as simple as a common mousetrap could prove fatal to Charles Darwin's theory of the origin of life through gradual evolution? Let me begin by quoting Darwin. In his famous book *The Origin of the Species*, he wrote:

> If it could be demonstrated that any complex organ existed, which could not possibly have been formed by numerous, successive, slight modifications, my theory would absolutely break down.[1]

Is there something about a mousetrap that leads to this absolute breakdown of Darwin's theory? We'll look at that in a moment, but first consider what a simple thing a mousetrap seems to be. If you look at the illustration below, you'll notice that a mousetrap consists of five pieces: a wooden platform, a hammer, a spring, a holding bar, and a trigger or catch.

What does this have to do with Darwinian Evolution? We turn now to biochemist Michael Behe's important new book, *Darwin's Black Box.*[2] Because even though a mouse-trap is a simple thing, it illustrates Behe's concept of "irreducible complexity." Here's his definition of this concept:

> By *irreducibly complex* I mean a single system composed of several well-matched, interacting parts that contribute to the basic function, wherein the removal of any one of the parts causes the system to effectively cease functioning.[3]
> A mousetrap is a good example.

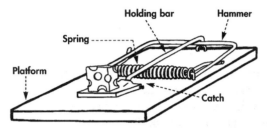

If a mousetrap is missing even one piece due to faulty manufacturing, which piece could be missing and still allow you to catch the mouse? The wooden platform? (No way to mount the trap.) The hammer? (The mouse could dance on the cheese all night long!) The spring? (The hammer would jangle loosely.) The holding bar or the catch? (You would have a sore thumb and no captured mouse!)

The point: The mousetrap is an irreducible system that will not accomplish its function if any one part is missing—"wherein the removal of any one of the parts causes the system to effectively cease functioning." The system will not function with one, two, three, or four components. You have to have all five working together. And not just together but with the right materials, the right shapes, and the correct placement to make successful function possible.

What has that to do with Darwin's theory that life evolved gradually through natural selection, through slow natural changes that increased the complexity of organisms over the expanse of millions of years? It is absolutely basic because, according to his theory, the driving force of evolution is "survival of the fittest" or "natural selection." Every small step leading to increased complexity of organisms must be either a neutral or a useful step—must not cause the organism to be less "fit." If it is less "fit," the organism likely would not be able to compete with those that are more "fit" and would die out.

Is it impossible to imagine any series of steps, all useful, that would lead to the complete mousetrap? A mousetrap could not evolve, piece by piece—*all five pieces must be present for the trap to accomplish its purpose.*

Are there vital functions in living creatures that require all parts and that could not be derived gradually by a series of useful more simple intermediates? Indeed there are! Behe gives compelling examples that point to problems with Darwin's theory.

How? This biochemist from Lehigh University in Pennsylvania pursued his molecular research with the query: Are there mousetraplike systems in the realm of nature that are irreducibly complex? Are there systems that could not have evolved piece by piece, each useful to the organism, until finally the complete complex mechanism was produced? If the answer is Yes then the present functions would never have developed and the organism never would have evolved.

Before we share some of his stunning exhibits, let us examine the biblical description of divine Creation in Psalm 33. It seems to me that Behe's work corroborates this description.

> By the word of the Lord the heavens were made, and all their host by the breath of his mouth. He gathered the waters of the sea as in a bottle; he put the deeps in storehouses. Let all the earth fear the Lord; let all the inhabitants of the world stand in awe of him. For he spoke, and it came to be; he commanded, and it stood firm (Ps. 33:6-9).

Incidentally, notice that this text describes the entire Trinity as being involved in the work of Creation. The word translated "breath" here is *Ruach* and is translated "Spirit" in Genesis 1:2. "By the word of the Lord"—instantly brings to mind the grand prologue to the Gospel of John, which majestically parallels Genesis' own great opening.

> In the beginning was the Word, and the Word was with God, and the Word was God. He was in the beginning with God. All things came into being through him, and without him not one thing came into being (John 1:1-3).

Who is this Word who created all things? Verse 14 says, "And the Word became flesh and lived among us." The Word is the preincarnate Christ who became Jesus of Nazareth. Thus Psalm 33 pictures the Trinity involved in the creation of life.

"For He spoke"—the emphatic pronoun is added in the Hebrew, setting God above any other mythological god that might claim creative ability.

"And it came to be"—literally, "it became" from the Hebrew root of Yahweh (I AM), the name of God. He spoke and it simply was! The old theologians used a Latin word to describe God's method of creation—*fiat* creation—a "let it be done" creation as in verse 9.

Think of what we have just read! According to Psalm 33, which is in perfect harmony with the Genesis 1 account, the Creator God created entire systems of life instantaneously by the command of His word. The Triune God created irreducibly complex systems that had to be designed, created, and placed in operation all at once or else the systems would not have functioned. Which is why I am intrigued by Behe's conclusion that there are some irreducibly complex biological and molecular systems that could not have evolved piece by piece. They had to begin designed, fully formed and in place, in order for the critical life system to function and the organism to survive.

Let us turn then to Behe's astounding and enlightening exhibits. I would highly recommend that you read his book. He has a gift for making the complicated simple, and he presents evidences of intelligent design that point out how unreasonable it is to believe that life has developed through evolution.

Exhibit one: The cilia

Cilia are microscopic hairlike structures on the surface of some cells. Some single-celled animals move via one or more cilia. Ciliated cells line the insides of our lungs, and the cilia move in unison, pushing foreign particles up to the throat where they can be swallowed. The male sperm has one long cilium that it uses to move itself toward the ovum. Cilia are tiny, but that does not mean they are simple. Behe describes a cilium as follows (you don't have to try to understand all of this, just notice how complex this seemingly simple structure is):

> The cilium consists of a membrane-coated bundle of fibers. The ciliary membrane (think of it as a sort of plastic cover) is an outgrowth of the cell

membrane, so the interior of the cilium is connected to the interior of the cell. When a cilium is sliced crossways and the cut end is examined by electron microscopy, you see nine rod-like structures around the periphery. The rods are called microtubules. When high-quality photographs are closely inspected, each of the nine microtubules is seen to actually consist of two fused rings. Further examination shows that one of the rings is made from thirteen individual strands. The other ring, joined to the first, is made from ten strands. . . . A protein called nexin connects each . . . double microtubule to the one beside it.[4]

Imagine yourself holding two flexible fishing poles upright in front of yourself. The two poles represent two of the microtubules within the cilium. They are only inches apart and are connected to each other by fish line at frequent intervals all the way to the top of the poles (representing the nexin fibers). Now, if you lift up one of the poles while keeping the other steady, the tops of both poles will bend—toward the right if you raise the left pole and toward the left if you raise the right pole. This illustrates how a cilium moves, with your arms serving as the "motors." The cilia also require motors to bring about their bending. The tiny molecular motors are called dynein.

A motor requires energy—electricity or gasoline for many motors with which we are familiar. The "gasoline" used by the molecular dynein motors is ATP (adenosine triphosphate). When ATP activates the dynein, one of the microtubules begins to slide past the other. The nexin fibers prevent it from moving far and cause the vertical motion to be converted to a bending motion. Of course, all nine double microtubules need to act in harmony for the cilium to move quickly and smoothly. Behe sees the complexity of this motion as clear evidence that life could not have simply evolved without some sort of master plan and master planner to design it and make all the parts work together so smoothly.

> All of these parts are required to perform one function: ciliary motion. Just as a mousetrap does not work unless all of its constituent parts are present, ciliary motion simply does not exist in the absence of microtubules, connectors, and motors. Therefore we can conclude that the cilium is irreducibly complex—an enormous monkey wrench thrown into its presumed gradual, Darwinian evolution.[5]

Remember, this is being written by a scientist who has changed his mind on the basis of the molecular evidence and has abandoned the theory that irreducibly complex systems can change gradually, or evolve! He now realizes that these systems must have been designed and placed into operation complete and functioning by something or someone.

And all this detailed structure is only one small part of a single cell! This is what Behe refers to as "Darwin's black box" because when Darwin was alive, he could not penetrate the deep secrets of the complexity of life—the technology needed to study the microscopic biochemical details had not yet been developed.

Behe in fact points out that cilia are of interest to scientists in several disciplines such as biochemistry, biophysics, molecular biology, and even medicine. In the past several decades, perhaps as many as 10,000 research papers dealing in some way with cilia have been published, but only two of these attempt to discuss the details of the evolution of cilia on the molecular and mechanical levels, and these two papers disagree!

> The amount of scientific research that has been and is being done on the cilium—and the great increase over the past few decades in our understanding of how the cilium works—lead many people to assume that even if they themselves don't know how the cilium evolved, *somebody* must know. But a search of the professional literature proves them wrong. Nobody knows.[6]

To add to the wonder, some bacteria have a whiplike structure (flagellum) that can rotate. The flagellum acts like an airplane propeller, whereas the cilium acts like an oar. Structurally, flagella are just as complex as cilia. They are another irreducibly complex system. Which brings up another question: Even if blind, random evolution were able eventually to construct one of these organelles (the cilium or the flagellum), why would it bother to make another entirely different complex system when it could get along with the first one?

Exhibit two: The eye

The eye is a classic irreducibly complex system that Darwin tried to explain. Instead of laying out a sequence of steps that would lead eventually from a very simple eye to the complex human eye, he discussed the eyes of various animals and suggested that natural selection could bring about gradual changes from the single-celled, light sensitive eyes of animals such as jellyfish to the concave grouping of light-sensitive cells in the eyes of the starfish to the ball of cells with a crude lens in the snails to the marvelous eyes of birds and humans.

In Darwin's thinking, evolution could not build a complex organ in one step or a few steps; radical innovations such as the eye would require generations of organisms to slowly accumulate beneficial changes in a gradual process. He realized that if in one generation an organ as complex as the eye suddenly appeared, it would be tantamount to a miracle. Unfortunately, gradual development of the human eye appeared to be impossible, since its many sophisticated features seemed to be interdependent. Somehow, for evolution to be believable, Darwin had to convince the public that complex organs could be formed in a step-by-step process.

He succeeded brilliantly.

Using reasoning like this, Darwin convinced many of his readers that an evolutionary pathway leads from the simplest light-sensitive spot to the sophisticated camera-eye of man. But the question of how vision began remained unanswered. Darwin persuaded much of the world that a modern eye evolved gradually from a simpler structure, but he did not even try to explain where his starting point—the relatively simple light-sensitive spot—came from. On the contrary, Darwin dismissed the question of the eye's ultimate origin: "How a nerve comes to be sensitive to light hardly concerns us more than how life itself originated."[7]

Now that we can look into the black box that biochemistry has opened, what does it reveal? Below is a simplified version of the details discussed in Behe's book. (Once again, don't worry if this all seems too complex to really understand. The point is that it is too complex to develop by accident.)

Light strikes the retina and reacts with a retinal molecule that immediately changes shape. The change in shape forces the protein rhodopsin, to which this molecule is closely attached, to change shape also. The change in shape of rhodopsin causes it to be attracted to a second protein, transducin. When that happens, the transducin drops off a small molecule and accepts a second slightly different one in its place. Transducin protein now binds to a third protein, phosphodiesterase, which has the ability to "cut" out a third molecule, which reduces the number of positively charged sodium ions. The resulting imbalance of positive and negative sodium ions inside and outside the cell membrane causes an electrical charge that is transmitted down the optic nerve and is interpreted by the brain as vision.

But what happens in the brain to then produce vision is a whole other marvel of complexity with which we cannot deal here!

Now that the black box of vision has been opened, it is no longer enough for an evolutionary explanation of that power to consider only the *anatomical* structures of whole eyes, as Darwin did in the nineteenth century (and as popularizers of evolution continue to do today). Each of the anatomical steps and structures that Darwin thought were so simple actually involves staggeringly complicated biochemical processes that cannot be papered over with rhetoric. Darwin's metaphorical hops from butte to butte are now revealed in many cases to be huge leaps between carefully tailored machines—distances that would require a helicopter to cross in one trip.[8]

Exhibit three: The bombardier beetle

Behe places another exhibit on display, this one being a favorite of creationists. Even I had heard about it long before reading Behe. This is an unattractive dark beetle only about half an inch long. However, it has distinguished itself by its unusual means of defense. Through an aperture in its rear end, it is able to blast scalding acid at its enemy. How is it able to maintain boiling acid in its body without damage to itself? The answer is that the beetle uses chemistry—the boiling acid is produced at the moment the creature jets its foul fluid. Simply, the process proceeds as follows:

Two chemicals, hydrogen peroxide and hydroquinone, are produced by special glands within the abdomen. They are stored together in a collecting vesicle. These two chemicals are capable of explosive reaction when mixed together but only under the influence of a special enzyme catalyst. Without the catalyst, the reaction between hydrogen peroxide and hydroquinone is too slow to accomplish what the beetle needs.

When danger approaches, the beetle releases into an explosion chamber the mixture that has been stored in the collecting vesicle. At the same time, the catalyst is squirted into the explosion chamber from surrounding glands.

> Now, chemically, things get very interesting. The hydrogen peroxide rapidly decomposes into ordinary water and oxygen. . . . The oxygen reacts with the hydroquinone to yield more water, plus a highly irritating chemical called quinone. These reactions release a large quantity of heat. The temperature of the solution rises to the boiling point; in fact, a portion vaporizes into steam. The steam and oxygen gas exert a great deal of

pressure on the walls of the explosion chamber. With the sphincter muscle now closed, a channel leading outward from the beetle's body provides the only exit for the boiling mixture. Muscles surrounding the channel allow the steam jet to be directed at the source of danger. The end result is that the beetle's enemy is scalded by a steaming solution of the toxic chemical quinone.[9]

Creationists have not always been careful in their use of this illustration. Richard Dawkins of Oxford University, in his book *The Blind Watchmaker*, an important book in defense of evolution, taunts creationists and makes the evolution of the ability of the bombardier beetle appear like a reasonable probability by indicating that both hydrogen peroxide and various quinones are used for other purposes in body chemistry.[10] The bombardier beetle puts to use for its protection what was already available.

> Dawkins's explanation for the evolution of the system rests on the fact that the system's elements "happened to be around." Thus evolution might be *possible*. But Dawkins has not explained how hydrogen peroxide and quinones came to be secreted together at very high concentration into one compartment that is connected through a sphinctered tube to a second compartment that contains enzymes necessary for the rapid reaction of the chemicals.[11]

To say the complex defense mechanism of this beetle came about because the necessary substances are used elsewhere in the body is like saying an automobile can develop in an auto wrecking yard because all the necessary parts can be found elsewhere in the yard. The fact is, this little animal has an interesting irreducibly complex mechanism that cannot function unless several substances and structures are present in the right configurations and at the right time.

Exhibit four: Blood clotting

One of the most intricate systems in the body of an animal is the process of blood clotting. Frequently, we pay little attention to a small scratch or cut that stops bleeding quickly. We are unaware of the miracle of design that causes the bleeding to stop. When we stop to think about it, we recognize that certain things have to happen for this system to work without damage to the whole body. (1) A blood clot must form to stop the blood flow. (2) The clot must form in the right place, otherwise it could block passage of blood in critical areas. (3) It must form at the right time. (4) The clot must be strong and well enough anchored to withstand the force of a system under pressure.

Behe refers to the blood-clotting system as a cascade, like a row of falling dominoes, a series of events leading to the desired end. The complexity involves names like fibrinogen, thrombin, accelerin, proaccelerin, glutamate residues, kallidrein. As laypeople we don't need to know all these terms, but reading about the complexity of the clotting process can help us realize that such a thing gives evidence of having been created by design, not accident.

When an animal is cut, a protein called Hageman factor sticks to the surface of cells near the wound. Bound Hageman factor is then cleaved by a protein called HMK to yield activated Hageman factor. Immediately the activated Hageman factor converts another protein, called prekallikrein, to its active form, kallikrein. Kallikrein helps HMK speed up the conversion of more Hageman factor to its active form. Activated Hageman factor and HMK then together transform another protein, called PTA, to its active form. Activated PTA in turn, together with the activated form of another protein . . . called convertin, switch a protein called Christmas factor to its active form. Finally, activated Christmas factor, together with antihemophilic factor (which is itself activated by thrombin in a manner similar to that of proaccelerin) changes Stuart factor to its active form.[12]

If you are able to follow and understand the above, you are probably a blood specialist! I include the paragraph only to impress you with the complexity of this system. And this is a description of only part of the system.

After the blood has been stopped, the healing begins. The growth of new cells is also tightly under control. The right kind or kinds of cells must be produced, only the right number of each kind as needed, and the cells must unite to produce tissue of the same shape as required by the location of the cut or wound.

What then are Behe's inescapable conclusions, based on this biochemical evidence? He invites the reader to:

Imagine a room in which a body lies crushed, flat as a pancake. A dozen detectives crawl around, examining the floor with magnifying glasses for any clue to the identity of the perpetrator. In the middle of the room, next to the body, stands a large gray elephant. . . .

There is an elephant in the roomful of scientists who are trying to explain the development of life. The elephant is labeled "intelligent design." To a person who does not feel obliged to restrict his search to unintelligent causes, the straightforward conclusion is that many biochemical systems were designed. They were designed not by the laws of nature, not by chance and necessity; rather, they were planned. The designer knew what the systems would look like when they were completed, then took steps to bring the systems about. Life on earth at its most fundamental level, in its most critical components, is the product of intelligent activity. . . .

In the face of the enormous complexity that modern biochemistry has uncovered in the cell, the scientific community is paralyzed. No one at Harvard University, no one at the National Institutes of Health, no member of the National Academy of Sciences, no Nobel prize winner—no one at all can give a detailed account of how the cilium, or vision, or blood clotting, or any complex biochemical process might have developed in a Darwinian fashion. But we are here. Plants and animals are here. The complex systems are here. All these things got here somehow: if not in a Darwinian fashion, then how?[13]

There it is—Behe's convincing case for an intelligent designer; unnamed and unsought but, like the elephant, too obvious to overlook. In fairness to Behe, we must emphasize that he is not promoting belief in a Creator God. He simply suggests that an intelligent designer designed a complete cell, replete with DNA codes, and placed that cell, with all the necessary systems for reproducing itself, at the beginning of the evolutionary journey. Nevertheless, his point remains—an intelligent designer, no less complex than the object designed, had to get the irreducibly complex systems started in the first place.

How should Christian thinkers respond to these biochemical conclusions? I can't speak for you, but I must tell you that my own mind and heart were thrilled with the information in Behe's book. As a creationist who believes that life has been on this earth only a short time, I set aside his *a priori* belief in billions of years for the evolution of life forms. But his brilliant defense of intelligent design on the molecular level of life was most satisfying to me. Behind all of this I see the great I AM. "In the beginning God created the heaven and the earth" (Gen. 1:1). "For he spoke and it came to be, he commanded, and it stood fast" (Ps. 33:9). Irreducible systems of complexity could never have come into being by evolution or chance. A Master Designer spoke them into existence.

Can we correlate our biblical faith with this scientific information? Oh, yes we can! Would you be surprised to learn that the Bible predicted this kind of undeniable evidence 2000 years ago? The brilliant Christian thinker named Paul wrote that you and I have all the evidence necessary to conclude that there is an intelligent design and, behind it, an intelligent designer called Creator.

> What can be known about God is plain to [men], because God has shown it to them. Ever since the creation of the world his eternal power and divine nature, invisible though they are, have been understood and seen through the things he has made (Rom. 1:19, 20).

To reject the overwhelming evidence from molecule to galaxy is to reject the very One who invites humans to seek Him, as we noted in chapter 1. "He that cometh to God must believe that he is, and that he is a rewarder of them that diligently seek him" (Heb. 11:6, KJV). I would be "without excuse" (Rom. 1:20) if I were to reject belief in a Creator after seeing the evidence Behe and others present from living organisms.

I believe that *Darwin's Black Box*, unintentionally perhaps, corroborates, affirms, and vindicates the Christian's faith in fiat creation by a divine Creator.

With this in mind I can say confidently: Young Christian, *Do not jettison your faith. Reason does not demand it.* Longtime believer, *Do not abandon your Bible.* Skeptic, *Please reconsider the evidence.* The cutting edge of this scientific evidence for design declares that an *a priori* belief in our Creator has strong support.

If God could design the infinite intricacies of the molecular systems within you, then can He not also design the infinite details of the life forces around you? Maybe you feel like your life is irreducibly complex right now. So complex, so chaotic, that you can see no design, no master plan in all the hurt, pain, and loneliness, all the insecurity and failure you feel today. Perhaps you feel your life is falling apart. If only there were Someone, somewhere, who was still in control. Someone who could speak a word of order and design and hope and life back into your private chaos. Someone who could take all those random, broken pieces and, with a word, put your heart back together again. There *is* such a Someone. To a paralytic young man consumed by his wretched guilt, Jesus spoke a word, "Son, your sins are forgiven" (Mark 2:5). To a broken woman consumed by her diseased hopelessness, Jesus spoke a word, "Daughter, your faith has made you whole" (Mark 5:34). He spoke a word that embraced the man, He spoke a word that caressed the woman. And He created them both all over again. "He spoke, and it came to be; he commanded, and it stood firm" (Ps. 33:9).

Remember, the Latins called it *fiat* creation. Creation by the power of His Word. But they also had another word for His creation: *ex nihilo* ("from out of nothing"). Because that is what the Creator did in the beginning. Out of nothing He made a most beautiful something.

And great news—He still can! Thanks to His cross on Calvary, the same Creator can speak the same creative energy into your broken chaos right now. From out of nothing, He can make a most beautiful something out of you, out of your life right now, even today.

Martin Luther once said, "God created the world out of nothing. As long as you are not yet nothing, God cannot make something out of you."[14] Maybe it is time we admitted our nothingness and asked God to make a beautiful something out of the nothing we have left to bring to Him.

---

1. Charles Darwin, *The Origin of the Species* New York: Mentor Books, 1958), 171.

2. Michael J. Behe, *Darwin's Black Box* (New York: The Free Press, 1996).

3. Ibid., 39.

4. Ibid., 59, 62.

5. Ibid., 65.

6. Ibid., 69.

7. Ibid., 16, 18.

8. Ibid., 22.

9. Ibid., 31, 32.

10. Richard Dawkins, *The Blind Watchmaker* (London: W. W. Norton, 1985), 86, 87.

11. Behe, 34.

12. Ibid., 84.

13. Ibid., 187, 192, 193.

14. Martin Luther in Helmut Thielicke, *How the World Began* (Philadelphia: Fortress Press, 1961), 25.

CHAPTER FOUR

Can You Get a Big Bang Out of God?

Would you be surprised if there were a big bang tucked away in the Bible's first words, "In the beginning, God created the heaven and the earth"? Back in the 1920s American astronomer Edwin Hubble (the satellite-mounted Hubble telescope was named after him) made what one writer describes as "one of the most revolutionary discoveries of our century."[1] After months and months of tedious, meticulous observation of the midnight heavens, Hubble concluded that the universe is expanding. The distant galaxies are all increasing in distance from us and from each other.

Speaking of those galaxies, the *New York Times* carried this headline recently, based on reports from the annual meeting of the American Astronomical Society, in San Antonio. "Suddenly, Universe Gains 40 Billion More Galaxies." Astronomers now conclude that instead of 10 billion galaxies in our universe, there are in fact 50 billion!

In our galaxy, the Milky Way, our own sun is just one of between 50 to 100 billion stars. Now scientists say there are 50 billion other galaxies out there!

What Hubble discovered is that these galaxies are all moving farther apart. Let me illustrate his finding with a balloon. If I mark a few billion dots on a balloon, you know what happens to the dots when I blow the balloon up. The bigger the balloon grows, the farther apart the dots spread. Hubble's revolutionary discovery was that our universe is expanding, because his measurements showed that the distant galaxies were all getting farther from each other and from us.

Kitty Ferguson, a Julliard musician turned Cambridge science writer, explains this theory as follows:

> If this is true, and no-one today seriously contests it, then unless something has changed dramatically in the past, the galaxies used to be much closer together. It follows that at some moment in the distant past everything that we might ever be able to observe in the universe would have been in exactly the same place. All that enormous amount of mass and energy would have been packed in a single point, infinitely dense.[2]

Enter now the celebrated English astrophysicist, Stephen Hawking, author of the best-selling book *A Brief History of Time*. In his 1965 Cambridge University doctoral dissertation, Hawking focused on the relatively new idea of "black holes"—those massive stars that burn up all their nuclear fuel and collapse in on themselves under the force of their own gravity. They are said to be crushed into a point of infinite density and infinite space-time curvature from which no light can ever escape.

It's a mind-boggling theory physicists now are convinced is true. They call that collapsed point of infinite density a singularity. Hawking took that research and Hubble's theory of an expanding universe and began to work backward from our current state. He concluded that if we went back in time far enough, the universe would contract into a black-holelike singularity. By 1970 he suggested that the entire universe must have started with just such a point of infinite density!

Here is how science-writer Ferguson explains the big-bang theory:

> Everything that was to be the matter/energy of the universe that we might eventually be able to observe was packed together in a point of infinite density. Ten to twenty billion years ago (as "time" is measured in the space-time frame which was to follow), this "exploded." That was the Big Bang. To imagine the infinite heat of "time zero" of creation is as impossible as imagining the point of infinite density. To imagine the light of it is also a meaningless endeavor, because light as we are able to see it didn't exist. After a time matter, instead of radiation, began to dominate the universe. The universe expanded and cooled enough for electrons and nuclei to form stable atoms. Matter could begin coming together by dint of its own gravity, starting the process that would eventually lead to stars and galaxies and planets. Ten to twenty billion years after the beginning, we find the universe we know today.[3]

Can you get a big bang out of God? There are some who believe that the big-bang theory proves the existence of God and actually supports the biblical account of Creation—somebody had to start that initial singularity.

"In the beginning," to quote once again the first words of Scripture, "God created the heaven and the earth."

As a result of the big-bang theory of "singularity," some would now read Genesis 1:1 like this:

> In the beginning, God created everything that was later to become what we now call the Heavens and the Earth, as well as the laws that direct that outcome, and God caused it all to begin happening.[4]

Can you get a big bang out of God? Perhaps you can. The biblical account of Creation would not be denied if you did! However, if, along with the big-bang theory, you conclude that God began life in this universe in the same way (energy and matter exploding into existence and radiating out from a singular point), if from a singular point God created a microscopic life form and then turned it loose to develop by evolution, or if a Creator God did indeed create the major types of organisms but stretched the process out over many thousands or millions of years, you are destined to ultimate, great disappointment. The Scriptures give no support whatsoever for a theory of divine creation of life over billions of years. I find no scriptural support for the theories that today are known as Theistic Evolution and Progressive Creation.

These are ingenious theories, for they attempt to blend together the ideas in Charles Darwin's *The Origin of Species* and God's *Genesis* account of Creation. Simply put, these theories declare that God is the creator of life but that the great variety of living forms came not by fiat creation but by slow evolution over billions of years, or that God spread His creative acts over long geological ages. Theistic evolutionists are even willing to have God carefully nurture the evolution process over the billions of years, protecting the growing cells, and even nudging them into productive cycles of natural selection. Those who promote progressive creation are willing to allow for six literal days of Creation, but they place great ages between the days. But neither the theistic evolutionists nor the progressive creationists are willing to accept the historicity and literal veracity of Genesis, chapters 1 and 2. Those chapters, they tell us, are not to be taken literally but rather are like parables and stories that teach vital truths but do not depict actual events. Theistic evolutionists believe the Bible tells us *Who* created, but Darwinian evolution tells us *how* He created.

Earnest efforts have been made to integrate scientific evidence as interpreted by the philosophy of naturalism with divine fiat Creation as portrayed in the accounts of Genesis. But as so often happens, those who strive to be accepted in both worlds end up being rejected by both worlds.

Return with me to the biblical world of the Creation account in Genesis 1. I will be the first to confess that I cannot prove that the biblical theory of origins is true. None of us was there "in the beginning"—not Moses who wrote Genesis (which is truly a brief history of time), not Stephen Hawking who wrote the book *A Brief History of Time*, not you, not me, not anyone. Only God was already there "in the beginning." Therefore, only God (and obviously now I am operating on the biblical *a priori* creationist point of view) knows the truth about what really happened "in the beginning." Rather than proving a theory of origins, what I would like to do with you is to examine the utterly untenable position of theistic evolution and progressive creation in respect to the overwhelming biblical evidence.

But before examining the biblical evidence, here is an important caveat: God did not write Genesis! Nor did He intend Moses to write it as a scientific textbook. This is not to say that Genesis is not scientifically faithful, but it was never intended to be a scientific text. Consequently, for Christian thinkers and scientists, the actual account of Creation is agonizingly brief. As I have read again the Genesis account and other biblical texts and as I have read other authors who attempt to interpret Genesis and as I have visited with scientists, I have found myself wondering why God did not guide Moses to include just a few more details in the creation account. If just a few more words about chronological sequence and time, and perhaps a date or two had been included, all the debate within the Christian community and between Christians and the skeptical world would be eliminated! Or so we might think. But there's another factor to consider. God is dealing with the reality of a fallen human race, and He has granted the human mind the right to say No to Him no matter what the evidence might be.

How else could God be a God of love in this fallen world where every mind must eventually choose which side it wants to be on in this great struggle between truth and error, light and darkness—how could God be truly love and truly committed to our freedom of choice if we were forced by the evidence to conclude His rightful sovereignty in our midst? "We will not have this Man to rule over us," the crowds screamed long ago. (See Luke 19:14 and John 19:15.) They were exercising their God-given right to say No to Jesus at Calvary. And that right is still ours.

Even if Moses had been given the actual dates for Creation and the actual photographs of the Creation events, you and I have just enough inborn creativity and perverseness to come up with thirty-one scientific and philosophical and even theological reasons why the dates and the photographs are in fact not part of the actual Mosaic account but have been concocted by later scribal insertions. You think about it. Even if the photographs were included and the dates were printed in the margins by the hand of Moses himself, we would come up with reasons why that "evidence" is in fact unreliable.

You say, Ah, we wouldn't do that! Do you remember how the defense for O. J. Simpson reacted to the thirty-one different photographs of him in the infamous Italian designer shoes? They declared them all forgeries—all thirty-one pictures of Simpson standing there in those shoes. He denied ever owning a pair, and his lawyers declared them all to be fakes. If the defense at a trial can do that today, we could (and no doubt many would) do the same with whatever evidence God gave to prove that He did indeed create the earth and the life on it.

In one of the parables Jesus spoke, He had Abraham say to the rich man who, from beyond the grave, was begging Abraham to help his yet living brothers, "If they do not listen to Moses and the prophets, neither will they be convinced even if someone rises from the dead" (Luke 16:31). If we don't like what a straightforward reading of Genesis says but instead twist and warp the texts to achieve our desired meaning, we are in essence disbelieving Moses (the author of Genesis), and no amount of evidence (even the dead being raised) is going to help us.

In other words, no amount of evidence would be sufficient to prove to us today the truthfulness of the biblical accounts of Creation, if we didn't want to believe. Nobody was there. Except God. So whatever theory of origins we embrace, all scholars are agreed, we must accept it by faith—plain, simple faith.

Let us turn now to the biblical creation account:

In the beginning when God created the heavens and the earth, the earth was a formless void and darkness covered the face of the deep, while a wind from God swept over the face of the waters. Then God said, "Let there be light"; and there was light. And God saw that the light was good; and God separated the light from the darkness. God called the light Day, and the darkness he called Night. And there was evening and there was morning, the first day. . . . God called the dome Sky. And there was evening and there was morning, the second day. . . . And there was evening and there was morning, the third day. . . . And there was evening and there was morning, the fourth day. . . . And there was evening and there was morning, the fifth day. . . . God saw everything that he had made, and indeed, it was very good. And there was evening and there was morning, the sixth day. . . . Thus the heavens and the earth were finished, and all their multitude. And on the seventh day God finished the work that he had done, and he rested on the seventh day from all the work that he had done. So God blessed the seventh day and hallowed it, because on it God rested from all the work that he had done in creation. These are the generations of the heavens and the earth when they were created (Gen. 1:1-5, 8, 23, 19, 23, 31; 2:1-4a).

The Hebrew word for day is *yom.* It is used 1,480 times in the Hebrew manuscript, and whenever it is linked to a numeral, it always signifies a twenty-four-hour solar day. Ralph Waldo Emerson wrote, "God had infinite time to give us; but how did He give it? In one immense tract of lazy millenniums? No, He cut it up into a neat succession of new mornings."[5]

What do we know about the time aspect of divine fiat Creation? Genesis makes only two statements: "In the beginning God created the heaven and the earth." "And on the seventh day God finished the work that he had done." Here is how one commentator put it:

> To the question: When did God create "the heaven and the earth"? we can only answer, "In the beginning." And to the question: When did God complete His work? we can only answer, "On the seventh day God ended his work" (ch. 2:2), "for in six days the Lord made heaven and earth, the sea, and all that in them is, and rested the seventh day" (Exod. 20:11). [6]

Does this mean that all the scientific evidence is now explained and all the questions have now been answered? I appreciate the way this commentator responds:

> These remarks regarding the creation account are made, not in an attempt to close the discussion, but as a confession that we are unprepared to speak with certainty beyond what is clearly revealed. The very fact that so much rests upon the creation record—even the whole edifice of Scripture—prompts the devout and prudent Bible student to conform his declarations to the explicit words of Holy Writ. . . . *There is always safety within the protecting bounds of Scriptural quotation marks.* [7]

What does that last line mean? Is it suggesting that we throw out science in favor of Scripture? No, it is not! "There is always safety within the protecting bounds of Scriptural quotation marks" simply reminds us that when we wander far from the biblical account of Creation, we inadvertently place ourselves in a difficult theological position. Watch now what theistic evolutionists and progressive creationists end up with—all because they attempt to accommodate evolutionary theory and time!

The question is not whether God could have used Darwinian evolution to create the vast array of life forms on this world, as the theistic evolutionary theory suggests. Of course God *could* do it that way. The question is, *would* He, not *could* He? He can do anything He wants. But *would* He use billions of years to evolve or create life forms? Theistic evolution and progressive creation say He did. But what kind of God would He be, if He had?

According to the Darwinian theory embraced by evolutionists (including theistic evolutionists), life evolved through chaotic sequences of natural selection, whereby only the fittest creatures survived. Those less fit were eliminated, eventually supplanted or destroyed by competitors so that only the fittest continued into the next geologic age. Very simply put: Darwinian evolution relies upon an incessant life-death cycle over billions of years of time. Life-death, life-death, life-death, ad infinitum, for billions of years until finally the *Homo sapiens* emerged to master this earth. Such a theory assumes that the hand of God allowed all of this suffering and dying to go on, even before sin cursed the planet.

Those who believe in progressive creation have similar problems. If the fossils represent the preserved remains of creatures God created periodically during the passage of millions of years, then we must explain some difficult problems. Why do these fossils, created long before Adam and Eve came into being and long before they even sinned, show signs of disease, parasites, and predators? If these creatures died millions of years before our first parents sinned, how can we explain the clear declaration of Scripture that death is the result of sin?

If God was the One who started the process billions of years ago and guided it through the eons, we are forced to believe that God used brutal pain and brutal death to finally achieve the evolution of humans. And all of this before humankind appeared on earth and before Adam and Eve sinned. There is no way, scientific or theological, to sanitize this theory of bloody cycles of life, pain, and death.

I repeat, the question is not *could* God have; the question is, *would* God have resorted to theistic evolution or progressive creation if He is the loving Creator that the Scriptures say He is? In my own humble observation, it appears to me that those who opt out of the biblical Creation account of divine fiat Creation in seven literal, sequential days in favor of a prefall, presin cycle of life and death have a most unenviable task of trying to explain the character of a loving God. What kind of God would subject His Creation to brutal death before there was even rebellion? Add to that this question: What kind of God is He who hides the truth about his life-death cycle inside a fable or myth that obviously teaches that death results only from intelligent rebellion against the Source of life? If death was part of God's original Creation plan (which He called "very good"—Gen. 1:31), why would the apostle Paul call death an enemy and say it would be destroyed?

Bertrand Russell, well-known as one who rejected

belief in God, was right when he pointed out the fallacy of theology that tries to accommodate itself to evolutionary theory:

> Religion, in our day, has accommodated itself to the doctrine of evolution. . . . We are told that evolution is the unfolding of an idea which has been in the mind of God through out. It appears that during those ages . . . when animals were torturing each other with ferocious horns and agonizing stings, Omnipotence was quietly waiting for the ultimate emergence of man, with his still more widely diffused cruelty. Why the Creator should have preferred to reach His goal by a process, instead of going straight to it, these modern theologians do not tell us.[8]

David Hull makes the point just as clearly:

> [The] process is rife with happenstance, contingency, incredible waste, death, pain and horror . . . the God implied by evolutionary theory and the data of natural history . . . is not a loving God who cares about His productions. He is . . . careless, indifferent, almost diabolical. He is certainly not the sort of God to whom anyone would be inclined to pray. [9]

What have we made Genesis and God out to be? Have we created Him in our own image? If God really took five billion years to create humans, why did He tell us He took six days? Does God lie in order to tell the truth? To those who respond by suggesting that God was simply accommodating the simple minds of the original readers, then what shall we say about Moses, the author of Genesis and regarded by many as one of the most brilliant minds in human history? Is it not the height of arrogance to assume we are brighter than our ancestors?

But if God does lie in order to tell the truth, do you want to go home to live with Him? Belief in theistic evolution or progressive creation turns Genesis into a fable. It makes Jesus and Paul, as well as Moses, naive knaves for passing on the myth. It means that the truth comes from Darwin rather than from Moses.

Accepting these nonscriptural interpretations of Creation raises other important questions as well. For instance: Was the method God chose for creating earth the same method He used in creating all intelligent life in the universe? Will His saints have to wait billions of years while He uses this method in the ultimate re-creation of this earth after the elimination of sin? How did He create the angels? Are they also the result of some sort of celestial life-death cycle? If so, then who could blame Lucifer for rejecting the sovereignty of the Creator who chose such harsh methods for creating intelligent life?

Oh no, some might protest, God did not do that with the rest of the universe—He only did that with us. Dear reader, in the holy name of God, why would the Creator resort to such a strange and bloody method for the Creation and bringing into existence of a being after His own image? Why would He resort to such laborious and slow methods of creation when, while here on earth, Christ exercised His creative power in instantaneous miracles and healing?

Enough wondering. Let the Bible interpret itself. "Therefore, just as sin came into the world through one man, and death came through sin, and so death spread to all because all have sinned" (Rom. 5:12).

When does the Bible declare that sin and death entered into the perfection of this planetary system? At the fall of Adam. Ever since the fall of Adam and Eve, what does all creation long for?

> The creation was subjected to futility, not of its own will but by the will of the one who subjected it, in hope that the creation itself will be set free from its bondage to decay and will obtain the freedom of the glory of the children of God (Rom. 8:20, 21).

According to the book of Romans, decay and death were not on this planet before the fall of the human race, but since that fall all of created life groans and longs for deliverance that only the returning Creator will be able to bring to us!

My friend, can you see that if you abandon the Genesis creation account in favor of long-ages creation or gradual evolution, you also have to abandon belief in the biblical teaching on the fall of man, the entrance of sin, and the promise and purpose of the Saviour. Furthermore, if the life-death cycle preceded and led up to the evolutionary creation of humanity—be it by God or by Darwinism—then Lucifer wasn't lying when he said that death is not the result of sin!

Now you know why I feel so deeply that we must not abandon the book of Genesis or the God of Creation.

I want to close this chapter with a story that my friend Jim Tucker tells in his wonderful book of nature, *Windows on God's World*.

Eugene Marais, South African naturalist, observed that a troop of baboons always slept in a cave situated at the end of a ledge high on the sheer face of a cliff. To get to the cave, the animals had to make their way along the narrow ledge that was only six inches wide in some places.

Because it was so difficult to reach, the cave was an extremely safe spot to spend the night and only one or two sentinels were needed to guard the sleeping troop.

One evening Marais noticed a leopard below the ledge as the baboons were approaching the cave entrance. The leopard was quite capable of making his way along the ledge if he chose to do so, and, with a few quick swipes of a powerful paw, could have his pick of the sleeping baboons. The leopard spotted the troop and began to stalk them, staying just below the baboons as they wound their way up the cliff. However, the baboons also spotted the leopard and Marais watched as two of them very stealthily made their way back along the ledge until they were directly over the big cat. Concentrating on the moving troop, the leopard was unmindful of the two individuals stationed above him.

Suddenly, the two baboons dropped onto the leopard, one biting into the cat's spine and the other lunging for his throat. In two swift movements the leopard grasped the baboon on his back in his jaws and ripped the other one open with his claws. Both baboons were killed instantly, but their actions saved the rest of the troop. The leopard was also soon dead, for the baboon that had attacked his throat had punctured his jugular vein. [10]

Darwinian scientists find it hard to account for the self-sacrificing behavior seen in some animals. They attempt to explain away any altruism because such behavior does not agree with the law of survival of the fittest—every man (baboon) for himself. Some endeavor to ex-

plain it as "group selection"—where one animal sacrifices itself for the sake of the nation of animals. Others
describe it as "kinship selection"—whereby the animal
sacrifices itself to preserve the survival of its genes in its
offspring. May I suggest another explanation? Could it
be that the heart of a loving Creator is implanted in the
life of His Creation?

> What then are we to say about these things? If
> God is for us, who is against us? He who did not
> withhold his own Son, but gave him up for all of
> us, will he not with him also give us everything
> else? . . . For I am convinced that neither death,
> nor life, nor angels, nor rulers, nor things present,
> nor things to come, nor powers, nor height, nor
> depth, nor anything else in all creation, will be
> able to separate us from the love of God in Christ
> Jesus our Lord (Rom. 8:31, 32, 38, 39).

1. Kitty Ferguson, *The Fire in the Equations* (Grand Rapids: Wm. B.
Eerdmans Publishing Company, 1994), 23.

2. Ibid., 23.

3. Ibid., 102.

4. Ibid., 127.

5. Ralph Waldo Emerson, cited in Howard A. Peth, *Seven Mysteries . . .
Solved!* (La Puente, Calif.: Lessons From Heaven, Inc., 1988), 1:181.

6. *Seventh-day Adventist Bible Commentary* (Hagerstown, Md.: Review
and Herald Publishing Association, 1978), 1:208.

7. Ibid. (emphasis supplied).

8. Bertrand Russell, *Religion and Science* (New York: Oxford University
Press, 1961), 73.

9. David Hull, "The God of Galapagos," *Nature,* vol. 352, 486.

10. Jim Tucker, *Windows on God's World* (Washington, D.C.: Review and
Herald Publishing Association, 1975), 169.

CHAPTER FIVE

A Blind Watchmaker?

"Why Sex?"

The question is posed in the title of an article I clipped from the popular science magazine *Discover.* The heading for the article went on to point out that: "[Sex] is evolution's single most important and perplexing riddle." Here's how Gina Maranto and Shannon Brownlee describe the riddle of sex.

Sex is an inefficient, risky way for an organism to reproduce itself. This may be surprising, even startling, to most people. But it is the long held, if little known, view of many biologists who are now trying to find out why sex evolved and, more important, why it has persisted and even flourished for at least half a billion years.

Sex, the scientists say, requires an inordinate amount of time and energy. And its main effect, providing offspring with a diverse genetic inheritance, is not, as many believe, a guarantee that some members of a species will survive during

71

times of drastic environmental change. Because sex diminishes a parent's genetic tie to its off-spring, it contradicts a basic biological tenet: that the main goal of an organism is to transmit as many of its genes as possible to the next generation. In fact, sex dictates that a parent can pass on only half its genes to each of its progeny.

Asexual reproduction (without sex) seems a likelier choice for nature to make. It is faster and more efficient, and it allows a creature both to rep-licate itself without the bother of mating, and to produce offspring that carry all of its genes. If by some fluke sex happens to arise in a species, theo-retically it should not take hold, the sexual crea-tures should soon be supplanted by the original asexual stock.

Says George Williams, a population biologist of the State University of New York at Stony Brook, "At first glance, and second, and third, it appears that sex shouldn't have evolved." Indeed, the persistence of sex is one of the fundamental mysteries in evolutionary biology today.[1]

Did you catch that last line? "The persistence of sex is one of the fundamental mysteries in evolutionary biol-ogy today." As Graham Bell, a geneticist at McGill Uni-versity in Montreal, put it, "Nobody's got very far with the problem of how sex began. . . . It's buried in the rocks."[2] Which means, we don't know! John Maynard Smith of the University of Sussex in England put it this way, "One is left with the feeling that some essential fea-ture of the situation is being overlooked."[3] I agree! So let me repeat the conclusion of this article: "Indeed, the per-sistence of sex is one of the fundamental mysteries in evolutionary biology today."

Why? Because the followers of Charles Darwin have a challenging time explaining not only the origins of sex but the rationale for natural selection's selections! What logical reasons can we find for nature's purported evolutionary choices? How did the two sexes originate? Darwin hypothesized that life evolved from a simple organism to more complex forms. But as the article noted, when we look at the simpler forms of life, we find no male, female differentiation. There are no male and female protozoans, no masculine and feminine amoebas. Most one-celled organisms reproduce by simply dividing into two. Therefore, how and why did the two sexes originate if reproduction without sex is more efficient?

Howard Peth asks a further question: "How could male and female sex organs that perfectly complement each other arise gradually, paralleling each other, yet remaining useless until completed?"[4] Would male or female organs half-developed be useful?

Because of problems like these, some scientists have come up with the "hopeful monster" theory, which proposes that megamutations (major changes) suddenly showed up one day and *surprise!* the organs are fully developed and ready to go! Let me remind you that the reproductive organs are composed of multiple, irreducibly complex systems (remember that phrase from Michael Behe's *Darwin's Black Box?*). Behe showed that a cilium is a structure of irreducible complexity. The male sperm has a whiplike cilium that allows it to move in its search for an ovum. The sperm with its cilium is composed and controlled by many intricate molecular structures and biochemical sequences that must all be present from the beginning in order for the sperm and the whip to function. Otherwise, the sperm would never reach the ovum and could not fertilize it.

Irreducible complexity applies to behavior as well as anatomy and biochemistry (as with the bombardier beetle). A good example dealing with reproduction concerns the instinctive behavior of mother dogs and cats who chew and sever the umbilical cord, remove the embryonic sack, and lick the newborn pup or kitten to stimulate circulation. If this behavior was not established and correct the first time, young pups and kittens would not have survived and dogs and cats would be unknown.

How does Charles Darwin explain the gradual evolutionary development of these reproductive organs and behaviors that clearly are perfectly complementary with the reproductive needs of the respective species? The answer is: He doesn't, because he can't. He tried, and his followers try.

Richard Dawkins, an Oxford biologist, wrote an influential book on evolution entitled *The Blind Watchmaker: Why the Evidence of Evolution Reveals a Universe Without Design.* [5] Next to *The Origin of Species*, many believe this to be the most significant book on naturalism and evolution.

The title of the book is a direct challenge to an eighteenth-century theologian named William Paley who defended the existence of God on the basis of design. Paley wrote about taking a hypothetical walk along the beach one day and stubbing his foot on a stone. Were he to be asked how that stone came to be there, he would probably answer that the stone had been there forever, and his statement would be hard to refute. But if, during his walk, he stubbed his toe on a watch lying among the pebbles and someone asked how it got there, he would give a different answer. The watch is too intricate, too precise an instrument. He would have to conclude that

. . . the watch must have had a maker: that there must have existed, at some time, and at some place or other, an artificer or artificers [a creative artist or artisan], who formed it for the purpose which we find it actually to answer; who comprehended its construction, and designed its use.[6]

That is Paley's famous argument for the existence of God. He is the great Watchmaker of Nature. All of nature is filled with "manifestation of design"—a design even "greater or more" than the design we find in a watch.

Richard Dawkins, an atheist, vehemently disagrees:

Paley's argument is made with passionate sincerity and is informed by the best biological scholarship of his day, but it is wrong, gloriously and utterly wrong. The analogy between telescope and eye, between watch and living organism, is false. All appearances to the contrary, the only watchmaker in nature is the blind forces of physics, albeit deployed in a very special way. A true watchmaker has foresight: he designs his cogs and springs, and plans their interconnections, with a future purpose in his mind's eye. Natural selection, the blind, unconscious, automatic process which Darwin discovered, and which we now know is the explanation for the existence and apparently purposeful form of all life, has no purpose in mind. . . . It has no vision, no foresight, no sight at all. If it can be said to play the role of watchmaker in nature, it is the blind watchmaker.[7]

Why is Dawkins so insistent on defending evolution? Let me add one more line: ". . . Darwin made it possible to be an intellectually fulfilled atheist."[8] Plain and simple, Dawkins *wants* to be an atheist—he doesn't want the divine in his life, and this makes him passionate for Darwin. The drive to be free of gods fuels evolution's drive to conquer all human philosophy and redirect all human thought.

But how do evolutionists handle the question of how sex developed as the method of procreation? In *The Blind Watchmaker* Dawkins spends twenty pages trying to explain it but ends up simply appealing to prior assumptions. He argues in and out and around the barn, but in the end he can offer little more than Darwin. Sexual reproduction and the factors that influence it are based on "a prior assumption rather than something to be explained in its own right."[9] Which is simply a scientific way of saying "That's the way it is, so that's the way it is, so don't ask questions." Which is the Darwinists loosely disguised way of admitting that they have no explanation for why sexual selection developed.

Parenthetically, it seems an enigma to me that an Oxford biologist can reference a "prior assumption" and be called a good scientist, whereas a creationist who believes in the Genesis account (also a "prior assumption") is called a "naive Bible thumper."[10] Indeed we all do have prior assumptions!

Ten years after Dawkins wrote his bestseller, Michael Behe came along and professionally—scientist to scientist—took Dawkins's defense of Charles Darwin apart. "In short, Dawkins's explanation is only addressed to the level of what is called gross anatomy. . . . Dawkins . . . merely adds complex systems to complex systems and calls that an explanation."[11]

It's the same thing as answering someone who asks how your stereo system was created by telling him you obtained a set of speakers and plugged them into an amplifier. Then you got a CD player and a tape deck and plugged them in as well. You haven't answered the question about creation and design. All you have done is explain how the complex systems—speakers, amplifier, CD, and tape deck—got connected together. You have not explained how they were designed and created. Behe's point is that Dawkins and Darwin have not told us how the various irreducibly complex systems got designed. They have simply plugged in all the components of the stereo system and expect us to believe that that is how a stereo system came to exist!

Behe writes: "Either Darwinian theory can account for the assembly of the speakers and amplifier, or it can't."[12] Behe (and inadvertently, Dawkins) has shown that it can't. Therefore, *the watchmaker is not blind*! And if there is a watchmaker, as Dawkins suggests, then who is this supremely intelligent designer?

> Then God said, "Let us make humankind in our image, according to our likeness; and let them have dominion over the fish of the sea, and over the birds of the air, and over the cattle, and over all the wild animals of the earth, and over every creeping thing that creeps upon the earth." So God created humankind in his image, in the image of God he created them; male and female he created them. God blessed them, and God said to them, "Be fruitful and multiply, and fill the earth and subdue it; and have dominion over the fish of the sea and over the birds of the air and over every living thing that moves upon the earth." . . . God saw everything that he had made, and indeed, it was very good. And there was evening and there was morning, the sixth day (Gen. 1:26-28, 31).

The biblical record is unequivocal. The human mind, the human body, the human spirit of male and female have been created together in the image of God by God Himself.

Human creative art is but the reflection of the image of God that resides within every human being. When a musician composes music, the process begins deep within that three and one-half-pound organ between the ears. He or she can hear deep within what no one has ever heard. As the song begins to grow within the consciousness, the brain then directs the fingers to grab a pencil (or a computer), and while the eyes watch, the fingers scribble away until intelligible symbols appear on a sheet of paper. Later, with that paper placed before the eyes, the musician is able to re-create the muscle actions in the fingers that result in the depression of the correct keys. If seated at an organ, the musician plays another keyboard with his feet and may join in singing at the same time. The whole is an infinitely complex process involving body, mind, and spirit.

Is such ability the result of random mutations operating over billions of years? Or have we in fact seen manifested in human flesh and art a fleeting reflection of the very spirit of God?

Human creativity is a reflection of the image of God!

So, too, is human sexuality—male and female—a crowning display of the divine image. It is not within the angelic race, for Christ himself declared that in heaven the angels neither marry nor are given in marriage. No other order of creation is able to procreate the image of God into additional intelligent life forms.

It is no wonder that Lucifer has turned such hellish fury against human sexuality! No wonder that on the sexual front of life the demonic powers unleash their most withering attacks against us! For it is our sexuality as expressed together in male and female that reveals the image of God upon this fallen planet. The Creator's signature is traced upon every leaf and every microscopic amoeba, but on earth His image can shine in no more glory than within the procreative powers of male and female together! Note carefully, neither male nor female alone is the image of God. It is in the union of male and female that the image of God in the human race is revealed, propagated, and completed.

And it is here that the true beauty of the divine plan shines through. For not only does the fact of sexual reproduction point to a Creator, the plan that He established in Eden illustrates His love and concern for His creation. For it is as we heed the instructions of God for proper relationships that we can fully blossom into His image.

Jesus Himself (Matt. 19:4, 5) ascribed these words to the Creator, "and they shall be one flesh" (Gen. 2:24). One-flesh sexual intimacy was created by God as a gift to the human race to be celebrated only within the protective confines of marriage between a man and a woman. There is no other way to read that verse. Neither sin nor God has created an alternate way for sexual expression within the human race outside of marriage between a man and a woman, a husband and a wife.

Darwinian evolution provides license for any sexual expressions in or out of marriage. Why should it matter? Evolution with its endless ages recognizes no Creator and no moral laws. Charles Darwin and Richard Dawkins are left without moral basis for defining or protecting human sexual expression. When they jettisoned the biblical creation account, they destroyed the only moral grounds for the protection of sexual expression.

Those who espouse evolution are forced by the logic of their theory to appeal to the survival of the fittest (not marriage) as the basis for protecting families. Their only alternative is sexual anarchy, whose horrific colors we are now witnessing unfurled in Hollywood's animalistic portrayals of violent human sexuality. Society today is reaping the sexual whirlwind of Darwin's theory.

We have tried in our fallenness to experiment with sexual alternatives to God's design described in Genesis, but it has not made our relationships any better.

Human sexuality is a gift from God that can teach us so much. I appeal to my young and not so young friends—human sexuality is a beautiful flower only to be shared and celebrated within the protective walls of a marriage between a man and a woman. Do you know why? Is God some mean and cruel tyrant trying to withhold something pleasurable from us? Not at all!

The reason God protects sex within marriage is because of the very truth that Darwin and Dawkins's evolutionary theory has obscured—God is a God whose highest expression of creatorship is found in His personal relationship with all of His Creation!

Creatorship calls for relationship. Our Creator is very big on relationships! He longs to protect you, and the gift of your sexuality, until that day when He leads you through your choices to someone with whom you can share the rest of your life. God knows that outside of marriage, sexual partnership can only produce a still-born relationship that in the end becomes destructive. For that reason, your Creator protects your deepest relationship by reserving it only for the very special marriage relationship. We must not break that holy special relationship with God that the unique intimacy of marriage enhances.

And to those who say, I don't want to get married! I respond, my friend, you don't have to get married. There have been noble men and women throughout the history of this race who have never married and who have made phenomenal contributions to human life and thought. If you wish to remain single, then remain like Jesus. His choice not to marry meant His choice not to share His sexual expression with any other human being. Was it easy for him? I doubt it! Hebrews 2 declares that He experienced the onslaught of all human temptation, so that he might deliver us from all evil. You have the right, just as Jesus did, to remain single and focused on your own life goals and dreams. The church affirms your choice and stands by you as your community of relationship where you may share spiritual, emotional, and social intimacy.

But if marriage is your desire, I promise you, it is worth the wait! Don't take my word for it. Let me share a letter I received some time ago from a student on the campus where I pastor.

> Thanks for responding to a question that had been pending in my mind for a long time. . . . I wish I could shout out to so many of the fellow students here on this campus. Please, stay away from sex until you are within the protective, loving boundaries of marriage. It hurts so much to realize that everything you could experience with your wife, in every God-inspired, imaginable way, you have already done with someone else, or a variety of people for that matter. It becomes the more painful as you marry a perfect virgin.
>
> The T. V. , for example, teaches us that sex is fun, and promiscuity is acceptable, and can be a

happy occasion. WRONG. I found, and firmly
believe, that God implanted a law in every human
heart, that we violate every time we enter through
the gates of life prematurely. I have yet to meet
the person that can tell me that having had sex
with a person he or she is not wedded to, was an
enriching experience.

God forgives, and I can now forgive myself.
However, the scars are still there and I will take
time to heal. The scars stay and the barren, empty
well of God-given sexuality takes time to fill up. I
would urge all the students here on campus to think
and go for the unparalleled, long term reward that
is awaiting them.

But perhaps you whisper, "I have not waited. I have
sinned and fallen short of the glory of God." Well, my
friend, welcome to the human race. But I have some very
good news for you. God does not only create. He re-cre-
ates as well. He still loves you and wants to be in a close
relationship with you.

That is why He was willing to die on the cross. He
died so that He might re-create every broken heart and
every shattered life. That Cross proves that no sexual fall,
no sinful failure can separate you from this love for He is
willing to give His very life to restore you to a positive
relationship with Himself. My friend, if today you feel
stained and smeared and sullied, take the broken pieces
of your heart to Jesus. If He could create the world in six
days, then surely He can re-create your heart with one
prayer.

A friend of mine who has found a friend in Jesus always scribbles a single reference beneath his signature,
"II Corinthians 5:17." Come to think of it—it's not a bad

way for us all to go through life: "So if anyone is in Christ, there is a new creation: everything has passed away; see everything has become new!"

---

1. Gina Maranto and Shannon Brownlee, "Why Sex?" *Discover,* February 1984, 24.

2. Ibid., 28.

3. Ibid.

4. Howard A. Peth, S*even Mysteryies . . . Solved!* (La Puente, Calif.: Lessons From Heaven, Inc., 1988), 1:111.

5. Richard Dawkins, *The Blind Watchmaker* (New York: W. W. Norton & Company, 1986).

6. Ibid., 4.

7. Ibid., 5.

8. Ibid., 6.

9. Ibid., 200.

10. Ibid., 316.

11. Michael J. Behe, *Darwin's Black Box* (New York: The Free Press, 1996), 38, 39.

12. Ibid., 39.

CHAPTER SIX

Jurassic Park and Noah's Ark

In the six hundredth year of Noah's life, in the second month, on the seventeenth day of the month, on that day all the fountains of the great deep burst forth, and the windows of the heavens were opened. The rain fell on the earth forty days and forty nights. . . . The waters swelled so mightily on the earth that all the high mountains under the whole heaven were covered; the waters swelled above the mountains, covering them fifteen cubits deep. And all flesh died that moved on the earth, birds, domestic animals, wild animals, all swarming creatures that swarm on the earth, and all human beings. . . . But God remembered Noah and all the wild animals and all the domestic animals that were with him in the ark (Gen. 7:11, 12, 19-21; 8:1).

None of us can fully comprehend the full significance of the passage above. Nevertheless, let us plunge into the deep together. Does the Flood story wash with the truth about God (theology) and with the evidence of science (geology)? To put it another way, is the Genesis account true to God and to science? What shall we do with the biblical flood story?

What we are about to examine is arguably the most controversial issue, the most hotly contested piece of evidence in the great debate between creationists and evolutionists. And so I want to share with you some of the research findings and studies that I have read, although there is still a library full of books I have not read. I am grateful for those who are bringing all their scientific and theological acumen to bear upon answering the hardest questions of all.

Note again the terse but dramatic account of the Flood recorded in Genesis, chapters 6 to 8.

> The Lord saw that the wickedness of humankind was great in the earth, and that every inclination of the thoughts of their hearts was only evil continually. And the Lord was sorry that he had made humankind on the earth, and it grieved him to his heart. So the Lord said, "I will blot out from the earth the human beings I have created—people together with animals and creeping things and birds of the air, for I am sorry that I have made them" (Gen. 6:5-7).

The God of the broken heart! Some parents know the meaning of that kind of pain. I was visiting with a father who called me long distance recently. He was concerned with his child, now grown but caught in a tangled and desperate web of trouble. I listened as that dad I had never met sobbed on the other end of the line for his child. No matter how grown up our kids, our heart breaks when their lives crumble.

Note again verse 6: "And the Lord was sorry that he

had made humankind on the earth, and it grieved him to his heart." I have known parents who agonized over their long ago choice to bring a child into this world. Had they known how it would turn out, perhaps they would never have created that life. There is no paternal or maternal pain that the broken heart of God has not felt too!

But the metaphor of God changes from a heartbroken parent to a desperate life-saving Surgeon.

> So the Lord said, "I will blot out from the earth the human beings I have created—people together with animals and creeping things and birds of the air, for I am sorry that I have made them" (Gen. 6:7).

In order to save a life, a surgeon may find it necessary to resort to drastic intervention—radical removal of diseased portions of the organism such as a lung, a kidney, or a stomach. The surgeon exterminates the diseased and incurable portion of the organism in order that he might save the rest before it, too, becomes contaminated, and he loses the entire life system.

God was faced with the surgeon's choice—and He made it, but it broke His heart. Will He destroy all? No. Verse 8 is clear. There is yet a portion of the dying organism that can be saved. If God can preserve that portion, He will preserve the human race.

> But Noah found favor in the sight of the Lord. These are the descendants of Noah. Noah was a righteous man, blameless in his generation; Noah walked with God. And Noah had three sons, Shem, Ham, and Japheth. . . . And God said to Noah, "I have determined to make an end of all flesh, for the earth is filled with violence because of them; now I am

going to destroy them along with the earth. Make yourself an ark of cypress wood; make rooms in the ark, and cover it inside and out with pitch. This is how you are to make it: the length of the ark three hundred cubits, its width fifty cubits, and its height thirty cubits. Make a roof for the ark, and finish it to a cubit above; and put the door of the ark in its side; make it with lower, second, and third decks. For my part, I am going to bring a flood of waters on the earth, to destroy from under heaven all flesh in which is the breath of life; everything that is on the earth shall die" (Gen. 6: 8-10, 13-17).

For the saving of the undiseased portion left of the human race, God designs a floating barge! I never realized the implications of the dimensions of the ark as depicted here in Genesis until I read John Whitcomb's book *The World That Perished*.

> The spatial dimensions of the ark constitute a remarkable testimony to the internal consistency and objective rationality of the biblical Flood account. . . . With regard to its proportions, "a model was made by Peter Jansen of Holland, and Danish barges called *Fleuten* were modeled after the Ark. These models proved that the Ark had a greater capacity than curved or shaped vessels. They were very seaworthy and almost impossible to capsize."
>
> Henry Morris, in a study of the stability of the Ark, has concluded that it would have to be turned completely vertical before it could be tipped over. . . . In every way, therefore, the Ark as designed was highly stable, admirably suited for its purpose of riding out the storms of the year of the

great Flood." As a flat-bottomed barge, not designed to move through the water, but simply to float, it had one-third more carrying capacity than a ship with sloping sides of similar dimensions.

Even more important, the dimensions of the Ark were sufficiently great to accomplish its intended purpose of saving alive the thousands of kinds of air-breathing creatures that could not otherwise survive a year-long Flood. Assuming the length of the cubit to have been at least 17. 5 inches, the available floor space of this three-decked barge was over 95,000 square feet, and its total volume was 1,396,000 cubic feet.

Such figures are difficult to picture without comparisons. For the sake of realism, imagine waiting at a railroad crossing while ten freight trains, each pulling fifty-two boxcars, move slowly by, one after another. That is how much space was available in the Ark, for its capacity was equivalent to 520 modern railroad stock cars. A barge of such gigantic size, with its thousands of built-in compartments (Genesis 6:14) would have been sufficiently large to carry two of every species of air-breathing animal in the world today . . . on only half of its available deck space. The remaining space would have been occupied by Noah's family, five additional representatives of each of the comparatively few kinds of animals acceptable for sacrifice, two each of the kinds that have become extinct since the Flood, and food for them all (Genesis 6:21).[1]

The actual dimensions are 300 by 50 by 30 cubits. A cubit is considered to be about 18 inches. The dimensions by modern units were 450 by 75 by 45 feet. The length was one and one-half times the length of a foot-ball field, and the height was equal to a building of four and one-half stories.

But the Flood story goes on. One hundred twenty pro-bationary years were provided for divine appealing to the dysfunctional and diseased human race. But finally the divine Surgeon could wait no longer.

If you read through the account of the Flood in Gen-esis 7 and 8, you will discover some important details about what happened.

1. It was global in its extent, meaning it covered all land masses at one time or another during the actual flooding: "The waters swelled so might-ily on the earth that all the high mountains un-der the whole heaven were covered" (verse 19).

2. All land and air creatures (except those in the ark) were destroyed and eventually buried by flood action: "Everything on dry land in whose nostrils was the breath of life died" (verse 22). This verse also makes it clear that "dry land" creatures were involved in destruction. Obvi-ously, some marine life and sea creatures would survive—even in a global catastrophe of this magnitude. Moreover, the passage above de-scribes a truly catastrophic cataclysm precipi-tated by exploding fountains of water from be-low as well as from above.

3. The occupants of the ark—both human and crea-tures—formed the new nucleus through which God repopulated the postflood earth. "But God remembered Noah and all the wild animals and all the domestic animals that were with him in the ark. And God made a wind blow over the

earth, and the waters subsided" . . . Then God said to Noah, "Go out of the ark, you and your wife, and your sons and your sons' wives with you. Bring out with you every living thing that is with you of all flesh—birds and animals and every creeping thing that creeps on the earth—so that they may abound on the earth, and be fruitful and multiply on the earth" (Gen. 8:1, 15-17).

The theological questions about the Flood seem answerable. For instance, Why would God destroy innocent creation? The fact that He is forced to so choose provides a clue that in the post-Edenic world the ravaging effects of the human Fall had penetrated the very heart of nature and creation. Who can know the mutant degeneration that sin sowed within the innocent heart of nature! God created this world and all of us with an intimate, intricate interrelationship so that in the beginning all life systems celebrated the glorious truth about God. He is a being questing for friends. All nature was masterfully designed by God to be intimately interrelated, because God is very big on relationships. When Adam and Eve fell, there may have been an immediate, simultaneous breakdown within them internally, perhaps even chemically, for guilt does produce chemical reactions within us. Our bodies do give off chemical responses—pheromones.[2]

Could it be that in the tragic fall of humankind there was a drastic chain-reaction breakdown of the entire ecosystem like a runaway domino chain, until all creation was tainted and twisted by the human Fall?

Consider also the probable role of Lucifer in the hellish production of mutant tooth and claw, fangs and poisons, thorns and thistles. Did he seize upon mutations and genetic aberrations and even become involved in genetic engineering, in order to call into question God's beneficent plan for our earth? The original Jurassic Park, which existed long before Michael Crichton's fictional creation, was the work of Satan. He filled it with raging, devouring dinosaurs! *Tyrannosaurus rex* is no figment of the imagination! But the production of horrible mutant creatures was terribly out of sync with God's original plan of interspecies harmony.

As a result of the Fall, the divine Surgeon was forced to excise the entire diseased organism, with the exception of the representatives of the species that were preserved within that giant floating barge.

There, in simple summary, is the Genesis account of the Flood. Does it hold up theologically? I believe the life-saving Surgeon paradigm makes this account very defensible in the light of God's character of relentless love.

But does the story hold up geologically? Geologists, scientists of the earth, have found fossils high on mountaintops and deep down in the earth's crust. These fossils are some evidence of prehistoric organisms.

Scientists call the vertical sequence of sediment and rock layers the *geologic column.* It is simply the vertical sequence of sediments beneath our feet. In the course of the history of this earth, millions of organisms have died, some of which have been buried and covered over to become fossils underground. Technically, the geologic column also includes those portions of the earth's crust below fossil-bearing beds, but in our discussion we are concerned with the natural progression of fossil remains that can be found in the upper part of the earth's crust.

You may be saying, "But what's the big deal? Of course we're going to find animal, bird, plant, and fish remains when we dig beneath the earth!" And you're right. But the very big deal is that whenever geologists find these remains, they are usually in the same vertical sequence or order. The deeper they dig, the older the rock formations become, and the simpler become the organisms embedded in the rock. When you get to the bottom, below which fossils are absent, you discover the very simplest (functionally and anatomically speaking) of all fossils. Or so it seems! Or to turn around and view this situation from another angle, the ordering of the fossils very nearly agrees with Charles Darwin's evolutionary theory—simple organisms in the oldest, lowest rocks becoming more complex on up the column until humans are the climax at the very top. This is precisely why most geologists, who have embraced Darwin's evolutionary theory—that all life forms evolved from a single shared ancestor—will point you to the geologic column and confidently declare that here is living (or rather dead) proof that the theory of long ages for evolution is true! How else can you explain how the simplest organisms are found in older, lower rocks and the more complex in the younger, upper rocks? The evidence is in the rocks, they maintain. You cannot argue with order of the fossils.

The point? If any piece of scientific evidence contradicts the biblical account of Creation, it would surely be this piece. The Genesis account teaches that God created all living things during a six-day Creation in relatively recent history. The geologic column, on the other hand, indicates that life forms, now found as fossils in ancient rocks, began as simple organisms and progressed during billions of years to complex animals and plants. Evolutionists believe that the geologic column proves that life evolved over long ages.

Does it? Are there other ways to explain the data? Most scientists who firmly believe in Creation do not challenge the predictable order of fossils in the earth's crust—it's there for all to see. But you also need to know that there are scientists who believe in the Genesis accounts of Creation and the Flood and who find that this belief offers an alternative interpretation of the geologic column.

The Geoscience Research Institute in Loma Linda is established to facilitate the study of science and religion issues (especially creation and evolution) by Christian researchers. They have published on the subject and will continue to do so as research progresses. I want to pass on to you what these scientists are exploring.[3] Because they believe that the Genesis account of Creation and the Flood are accurate history, they find that the fossil evidence from the crust of the earth fits well into a different scenario. Can they be accused of not having an open mind because they accept biblical authority? No. No more than the scientist who approaches the study of the earth with a previous belief in evolution.

They understand the sequence in the earth to be the result of ecology, hydrodynamics, and behavior of organisms in a global Flood. Their theory, called *Ecological Zonation,* suggests that the order in the geologic column was established by the order in which life forms died and were buried in the great Flood.

Simply put, these scientists are looking for evidence that affirms that the floodwaters, exploding from beneath and pouring down from above, covered and buried the simplest organisms first—those in the soil or at the bottom of the sea. As the raging waters grew higher and higher, they engulfed and drowned more and more creatures, many of them more complex. Naturally, mobile animals and reptiles and amphibians, as well as birds, would instinctively flee to higher ground. Also, animal carcasses, as well as trees and plants, would float for a time and would be buried later at a higher level. These scientists suggest that the geologic column was formed not by evolutionary ascent over long ages but rather by the sequential burial of plants and animals in their habitats by rising floodwaters, by the fleeing of animals to higher ground, and by the hydrodynamics of floating animals and plants in floodwaters.

If these scientists are right, the geologic column is a portrait, frozen in time and rock, of life forms fleeing rising waters and buried by a worldwide Flood. This would make the geologic column the result of a relatively short segment of time—not long geologic ages.

Geologists have a rule of thumb to guide them in determining the time it takes to lay down sedimentary layers and strata: Little water—much time; much water—little time. Using rates of erosion and sedimentation that can be observed today might lead us to conclude that long ages would be required to lay down the multiple layers such as one sees from the rim of the Grand Canyon—little water, much time. However, when you factor in a flash flood, the picture is radically changed.

Recently my attention was directed to a newly published book entitled *Faith, Reason, and Earth History* by Leonard Brand, chairman of the Department of Natural Sciences at Loma Linda University.[4] Note what he has to say:

> The average deposition rate in a modern flash flood, measured over one hour, is one million meters of sediment per thousand years (one thousand meters per year). This rate is 100 million times the average rate measured over one million years (0. 01 meters per thousand years). Consequently, if the flood water only equaled a modern flash flood continuously covering all the earth, it would take 8.4 months to deposit the existing Cambrian through Mesozoic sediments [an amount of material that evolutionist

geologists believe was deposited over a period of approximately 400 million years].[5]

Brand's point—a modern flash flood that extended over all the earth would lay down around 400 million years of the geologic column in 8. 4 months—much water—little time! This fits well into the time frame of the Genesis flood. So, is ecological zonation the solution to understanding the geologic column? Brand, and the staff of the Geoscience Research Institute, are careful scientists who make no sweeping scientific claims. They recognize exceptions and qualifiers as they explore the nature of the earth's crust and compare it with the biblical narrative.

Our current understanding of this hypothesis leaves many unanswered questions; but until a more satisfactory hypothesis is developed, ecological zonation is a place to begin the process of developing testable hypotheses for the ordering of the fossils.[6]

The geologic column deals only with the life forms found in the rocks. But how should we react when we hear that radiometric dating gives ages of billions of years for some of the rocks themselves? I have no difficulty accepting the creation by God of earth as an unformed geological mass long before He chose it as the site for the creation of plants and animals and the human race. We should not be bothered if radiometric dating methods reveal that this ancient rock in space is billions of years old. That does not change the veracity one iota of the Genesis account of a young earth Creation. Which is not to suggest that all radiometric dating is beyond dispute and without need for alternate interpretations today. Difficult questions remain in this area.

Perhaps more difficult for creationists than radiometric dating is the distribution of animals and plants, both fossil and living, around the world. What do we do with animals found on distant continents far from Asia Minor where the ark rested?

The question here centers around how animals got to where they are now found and why many species occur only in a limited geographical area. If their ancestors all migrated from one point, why don't we find them distributed worldwide? Particularly troubling are certain species in Australia and the tree-dwelling sloths of South America. The sloths cannot walk well on land but are geographically distant from the place where the ark landed.[7]

Did the God who supernaturally ordered these animals' entry into the ark also supernaturally return them to their original habitats? Who can know?

The point here is that there are still questions that we must wrestle with and answers that are not easily forthcoming. Let us not conclude from this discussion that accepting the biblical account of Creation and the Flood is an uncomplicated position to take.

Oh yes, Darwinism is faced with very perplexing questions also—and in the previous chapters we have examined some of these. The conventional view of the geologic column faces a serious problem. If this is an evolutionary sequence of animal and plant development, where then are the intermediate forms needed to form a continuous, smooth sequence from simple to complex? Why is the chain of life broken into many segments with no connecting links between the segments? The fossil order is strangely muted without any convincing evidence regarding its existence. Brand writes:

> Phylogenetic trees [diagrams showing the interrelationships between various historical and

modern species] in many textbooks and popular books show a complete tree all the way back to the beginning of life. Trees that show which parts are supported by fossil evidence and which parts are hypothetical are more interesting. Such trees show that the evolutionary connections between virtually all phyla and almost all classes are only theoretical. Non-interventionist scientists [those who reject the intervention of God in nature] are aware of this. Charles Darwin identified this as the greatest weakness in his theory. He believed the intermediates would be found. However most of the thousands of fossils that are found fall within the existing groups. As more fossils are found it becomes more clear that the gaps between major groups of organisms are real, and sequences of intermediates are not likely to be found.[8]

Thus, both creation and evolution have problems; both have to bridge their unsolved problems by faith. And so, in a world still filled with unanswered questions, how shall faith believe?

I can't answer for you, but I can answer for me. I'm going to believe the Book. I believe the Bible is authoritative in theology, science, and history when it addresses those topics, as it does with the Flood. I accept that record as inspired. Although I can understand why it has come under such withering attack!

If I were Lucifer, I would fight the Flood story with all my being for two very major reasons: 1. If the Flood story can be shown to be false, then it will follow *ipso facto* that the Creation story is also false. Because without the Flood, time—long periods of time—are needed to produce the geologic column. Without a flood, how else can you explain the ordering of the fossils in the geologic column? Animals caught and preserved in the rocks either evolved gradually (geologic time), or God's creative work extended over long ages (nonliteral days of creation). And so if I were Lucifer, I would do all in my power to erase the knowledge of the Genesis flood, for by so doing I would establish belief in geologic ages, which lays the foundation for the theory of evolution, which eliminates need for belief in a Creator.

2. If the Flood story can be shown to be false, then it not only eliminates further evidence of the Creator but also eliminates further evidence of an imminent divine judgment for the human race. Tut, tut, tut—God isn't going to judge this earth—"for all things continue as they have from the beginning" cry the skeptics (2 Pet. 3:4). But the apostle Peter goes on to give three examples that show that all things have not, or will not, continue unchanged from the beginning—Creation, the Flood, and the second coming of Jesus (2 Pet. 3:3-7). The cry of the skeptic is also Lucifer's strategic deception. You're not going to be judged for your life choices. There is no God. And even if there were, He would be too loving ever to do anything that radical. Come on—relax—not to worry—"all things continue as they have from the beginning." If I were Lucifer, I would know the New Testament backward and forward, and I would know that Jesus and the apostles cited the Flood as proof of the final, cataclysmic judgment on all sin. If I were Lucifer, I would know such a judgment would involve me! I would eliminate the knowledge of the Flood so that I could establish belief in evolutionary development over long ages and thus destroy a belief in Creation and in the Creator. I would also destroy belief in an imminent judgment. Put plainly, I would destroy belief in the Flood so that I could destroy belief in Creation so that I could destroy belief in the imminent judg-

ment of the earth!

But I am not Lucifer. I am a fallen sinner like you and like Noah. And like Noah, I with you want to find grace in the eyes of the Lord. How? Not in an ark made of gopher wood. But a cross made of olive wood. Just an old rugged cross. But like the ark, a wooden place of divine safety, divine salvation. It is there, in the embrace of our loving Creator, that we may find the refuge of grace in the storm of impending judgment. As the famous hymn says,

> Jesus, Savior, pilot me
> Over life's tempestuous sea . . .
> As a mother stills her child,
> Thou canst hush the ocean wild . . .
> Wondrous sovereign of the sea,
> Jesus, Savior, pilot me.

As the story ends—"But God remembered Noah" (Gen. 8:1).

------

1. John C. Whitcomb, *The World That Perished* (Grand Rapids: Baker Book House, 1988), 24, 25.

2. Some of these thoughts arose in discussions with Maelen Kootze and Clark Rowland, for which I wish to thank them.

3. Those wishing more information can write to the Geoscience Research Institute, Loma Linda University, Loma Linda, CA 92350.

4. Leondard Brand, *Faith, Reason, and Earth History* (Berrien Springs, Michigan: Andrews University Press, 1997).

5. Ibid., 218

6. Ibid. 279

7. This issue is discussed in Ibid., 302, 303.

8. Ibid., 173

CHAPTER SEVEN

Inadmissible Evidence

If this were a court of law and I were the defense attorney, I would endeavor to enter a piece of inadmissible evidence. You know what inadmissible evidence is, don't you? It is evidence the court will not allow to be entered—evidence illegally obtained, hearsay, or protected. Or evidence that is nonverifiable or nonpertinent to the case. But if I were the defense attorney, I would do everything humanly and legally possible to inject this very particular piece of evidence I have found into the court proceedings and the judicial record.

Do you know why I am passionate about entering this piece of inadmissible evidence? Because it is my deep conviction that the jury of public opinion could be, perhaps even would be, persuaded that my client has been right from the very beginning on the basis of this inadmissible piece of evidence.

Now I must inform you that the reason this piece of evidence is inadmissible is because the court of scientific opinion does not allow for it. This piece of evidence cannot be scrutinized by microscope or quantified by telescope. It cannot be verified by test tube or Bunsen burner. It cannot be arrived at by algebraic formula or geological observation. In short, it cannot be arrived at by the scientific method. Hence, it is not admissible before the bar of scientific opinion. Should I bring it up, it would occasion the cries of "Objection, your honor—objection, objection, objection," and I am fearful it would also receive the ruling, "Objection sustained" over and over again.

But in spite of the legal uphill maneuvering it would take, I would still explore every possible legal angle and pursue every potential statutory lead to discover a way to introduce this piece of evidence before the jury of public opinion. For if I could enter it before the court, I am convinced that the position I am advocating would be shown to be incontrovertibly true.

What is this piece of inadmissible evidence that I wish so very much to enter as we continue our journey through the great debate between Creation and Evolution, between the Holy Scriptures and Charles Darwin?

Ladies and gentlemen of the jury, I wish to enter the inadmissible piece of evidence found on the calendar hanging on your wall. You say there is nothing on the calendar that is significant to this problem. But therein lies the evidence: I hereby submit to the jury that the seven-day week and the seventh-day Sabbath are a perpetual testimony to the veracity and historicity of the Creation accounts in Genesis 1 and 2.

Allow me now to read into the record the evidence of the seven-day week and the seventh-day Sabbath:

> God saw everything that he had made, and indeed, it was very good. And there was evening and there was morning, the sixth day. Thus the

heavens and the earth were finished, and all their multitude. And on the seventh day God finished the work that he had done, and he rested on the seventh day from all the work that he had done. So God blessed the seventh day and hallowed it, because on it God rested from all the work that he had done in creation. These are the generations of the heavens and the earth when they were created (Gen. 1:31–2:4).

Do you realize that there is no historical or astronomical explanation for the existence of the seven-day week apart from the Genesis account of Creation? Let's take an astronomy quiz together, shall we? Let's find out how current we are in our scientific knowledge. In our solar system, what goes around every twenty-four hours? The earth turns once on its axis. What goes around every month or "moonth?" The moon circles the earth (the synodic month is actually 29.5 days long). What goes around every year, solar year, if you please? The earth makes one revolution around the sun.

Now, what goes around every week, every seven days? Access your scientific memory and recall what recycles every seven days? There must be something, because every other natural measure of time involves an astronomical cycle. What goes around every seven days? The answer? Nothing. The seven-day week, contrary to the day, the month, and the year, is tied to no astronomical cycle. Then where did it come from? Let us turn now from astronomy to history.

I went to the university library recently to research this question. There was a whole shelf of books devoted to the philosophy and history of time. One of the books I examined was Anthony Aveni's *Empires of Time*. He is

Russell B. Colgate, professor of astronomy and anthropology at Colgate University. Allow me to quote from this scientist as we seek evidence for the seven-day week:

> The word genesis means "origination," and every genesis myth begins with a sense of time. Our modern scientific genesis began more than ten billion years ago in a colossal explosion from which all events and things have spun. Usually implicit in every genesis is a purpose, though for many of us that original explosion had as little purpose in a human sense as anything in history.
>
> In the Judeo-Christian tradition of the Old Testament, the purpose of the creation stories in Genesis seems to be to demonstrate that all things were intended to be good. Perhaps all people need to believe in a world that can be conceived as orderly, intentional, purposeful, and as created specifically with them in mind—above all, a good world. Biblical Genesis satisfies that need by stating that God made it so. . . . Most biblical scholars regard Genesis to be an amalgam of myths brought together from a number of different sources.[1]

Wouldn't you know it—he brings up the book of Genesis, not as authority, but as simply a collection of myths. But I do not want to ask him about theology. He is a scientist, and I want to know what scientific foundation he has for the existence of the seven-day week. Note what he says:

> Any page of the wall calendar will reveal another subdivision to the time units Westerners have created: seven vertical divisions to the sequence

of numbered blocks, each column with its own name. The four or five horizontal bands, called weeks, into which we group the moon's days constitute a peculiar time division. There is no single celestial body such as sun or moon, no obvious natural cycle to which we can directly attribute this little packet of time. Moreover, many other cultures and traditions also tally an interval of about the same general duration in their calendars.[2]

Strange, isn't it? He allows that this "little packet of time" is found around the world in various cultures and traditions. But why does he offer an explanation?

Some biologists believe the week is self-determined. The 7-day biorhythm in the human body is one of the recent discoveries of modern chronobiology. It manifests itself in the form of small variations in blood pressure and heartbeat as well as response to infection and even organ transplant: for example, the probability of rejection of certain organs is now known to peak at weekly intervals following an implant.

We are not unique in broadcasting this beat: even simple organisms, down to bacteria and one-celled animals, seem to share it with us. There is, for example, a 7-day rhythm in the mermaid's wineglass, a species of algae whose configuration resembles a champagne glass with a long stem and a large flowery globe at the end. This organism can be entrained to reduce its rate of growth only when exposed to an alternating light-dark period of 7 days—no more, no less.

Amazing as it may seem, we were all created with a

seven-day biorhythmic cycle built into us—from complex humans to simple one-celled organisms! Do we wonder where that came from? Note Aveni's conclusion:

> Does social time entrain biological time? We might be able to connect the faint circa-septan, or 7-day, periods in our biological makeup to the week cycle upon which economically motivated human beings thrive. However, we know that the Romans, to whom we owe most of our temporal habits, worked on an 8-day cycle, the last day of which was a market day. Similarly, our word sabbath comes from the Jewish concept of the periodic recurrence of a day of abstention from work in the cycle—the seventh day—which the Jews gave over to the worship of the deity. So important was this round of the calendar that the most famous creation story in Genesis was built around the everyday structure of social time. The creation lasts 7 days—not 3 days or 6 months.[3]

As a scientist, Aveni is not willing to accept the idea that God placed the seven-day cycle in our body chemistry at Creation. But he cannot ignore the fact that this cycle seems to be a part of the natural world. He offers no explanation that fits the data as well as the idea that God created life to live on a seven-day cycle.

It is true that the histories of time that we read document variations in the length of the week from time to time throughout history. The Greeks experimented with a ten-day week (decade). The Romans went to an eight-day week. The French Revolutionary Convention during the French Revolution decreed a ten-day week in an attempt to totally rewrite history and reinvent time along a decimal system. It was abandoned when Napoleon came to power. The Soviet Union experimented with the week in this century. In 1929 they went to a five-day week, in 1932 to a six-day week, but by 1940 they had returned to the global seven-day week.

Where did it come from, this "little packet of time"? Ladies and gentlemen of the jury, the most conclusive evidence we have in history, philosophy, and science for the establishment of our global seven-day week is the ancient Hebrew account of the Creation of the world. Which leads me to repeat the assertion I made in entering this piece of inadmissible evidence: I hereby submit that the seven-day week and the seventh-day Sabbath are a perpetual testimony to the veracity and historicity of the Creation accounts in Genesis 1 and 2.

Science cannot explain the seven-day week, except by appealing to history. And history declares that the most consistent accounting for our present day seven-day week is found in the ancient Hebrew recording of Creation. Thus the seven-day week and the seventh-day Sabbath are a perpetual testimony to the veracity and historicity of the Creation accounts in Genesis 1 and 2. Not only do we have both of them affirmed here in the Creation accounts of Genesis, but we must also reckon with the indisputable linkage to these accounts in the very heart and soul of the divinely composed Ten Commandments.

> Remember the sabbath day, and keep it holy. Six days you shall labor and do all your work. But the seventh day is a sabbath to the Lord your God; you shall not do any work—you, your son or your daughter, your male or female slave, your livestock, or the alien resident in your towns. For in six days the Lord made heaven and earth, the sea,

and all that is in them, but rested the seventh day;
therefore the Lord blessed the sabbath day and con-
secrated it (Exod. 20:8-11).

Jacques Doukhan, professor of Old Testament and Hebrew at the theological seminary at Andrews University,
describes the fourth commandment as the geometric and
thematic hinge of the entire Decalogue—the very place,
by the way, where the seals were stamped in ancient cov-
enant documents.[4] The first three commandments describe our relationship with God, and the last six commandments describe our relationship with each other. And
in the middle, as a hinge between God and humanity, is
the Sabbath commandment that explains the basis of our
relationship both to God and to each other.

It is both a thematic hinge and a geometric hinge.
Sixty-seven Hebrew words are in the first three commandments. Forty-one Hebrews words are in the last six commandments. The center commandment is made up of
fifty-five words (which is one more than half of the rest
of the Decalogue of 108 words). Indeed, geometrically
and thematically this is the hinge of the Decalogue.

What is the message of this great heart of the Ten
Commandments? You already know. By the way, I remind you that Moses' eyewitness account of receiving
the Decalogue declares that God wrote these Ten Commands with His own finger on two tablets of stone (Exo-
dus 31:18). I don't know if it really happened the way
Cecil B. DeMille portrayed it in his epic film, *The Ten
Commandments,* where out of the fiery presence of the
divine, a hand emerges and carves in letters of flame the
Ten Precepts. All I know is that Moses, arguably the most
brilliant human ever to have lived, recorded that God
Himself wrote with His finger the entire Decalogue,

which includes the fourth commandment.

Doukhan reminds us that only two of the Ten Commandments are "positively formulated"—meaning these two do not begin with the familiar negative prohibition, "Thou shalt not." Significantly, they are juxtaposed together in the heart and along the hinge of the Decalogue. "This correspondence," Doukhan writes, "indicates a common concern." "Remember the Sabbath day" and "honor your father and your mother." What do they have in common? Both are calls for us to remember our origins and our roots as human beings. The fourth commandment calls us to remember our origin in "the creative act of God," and the fifth commandment enjoins us to remember our roots through "the procreative actions" of our parents. Both center commandments were given to protect the truth about our human origins! Honor your mama and papa, who procreated you. And Remember the Sabbath of the Lord your God, who created you!

At the heart of all truth is the truth about our origins! It is the truth at the heart of the Creation account. It is the truth at the heart of the Decalogue. And so, we emphasize again, it must be stated that the seven-day week and the seventh-day Sabbath are a perpetual testimony to the veracity and historicity of the Creation accounts in Genesis 1 and 2.

Let us now go even further. I say humbly but boldly to my evangelical friends who are reading this book, whether Protestant or Catholic: The only biblically consistent way one can reject the validity of the seventh-day Sabbath is to reject the veracity of the Creation account in Genesis 1 and 2.

Pope John Paul II was being utterly consistent recently with his tradition that rejects the validity of the seventh-day Sabbath when he announced to the scientific community on October 22, 1996, at the Pontifical Academy of Sciences, that while the evolutionary theory might be the best explanation for the existence of the human body, Rome would still insist that the human soul itself came from God. What he was saying was that the church would not argue against evolution of the body through long ages, as long as we recognize that God placed the soul within the body. It's as if he said to scientists, "You may have the body but you cannot have the soul!"

I cannot agree with him in his surrender of the biblical account of how our bodies came into being. But I recognize that his position is consistent with his rejection of the seventh-day Sabbath of the Creation account and the Ten Commandments. If Genesis 1 and 2 are a historical myth, then it logically follows that the basis of the seventh-day Sabbath (a seven-day Creation) and the fourth commandment (which references the seven-day Creation) have been utterly destroyed.

This presents a most disturbing problem for the evangelical community of America that has fought so hard to defend biblical creationism on the basis of Genesis 1 and 2. On what logical basis can my evangelical friends champion the truth of Creation, when they in the same breath reject the seventh-day Sabbath as a memorial of Creation? Why battle for Creation when you have abandoned God's memorial of Creation?

Such a position is both illogical and inconsistent. You might as well proclaim the Genesis account a myth as the pope did and embrace Sunday as Rome's alternative to the divine Sabbath. Biblical consistency absolutely will not allow any other choice. Therefore, I appeal to my Protestant and Catholic Bible-believing, Creator-trusting, friends: Please reexamine for yourselves God's teaching regarding His gift of the seventh-day Sabbath to the entire human race from the very beginning of Creation and time.

I remind my readers that if the Sabbath had always been remembered and the Creator worshiped on His holy day, there never would have arisen Charles Darwin with scientific atheism and Karl Marx with political atheism. Human civilization has reaped the whirlwind of forgetting to remember the Sabbath day of our Creator.

And as Christians, what logical leg do we have to stand on, in our quest to share biblical truth with others, if we ourselves reject the veracity of the Genesis account? If we throw out that one piece, which is foundational to our understanding of ourselves and our place in the universe, sooner or later we will abandon all belief in divine revelation, and the Bible will become just another book of myths to us.

After this detailed and earnest look into the heart of Creation, I am convinced that, in fact, the biblical truth about Creation is the very foundation of all revealed truth.

But what about all the scientific evidence? you ask. My friends, science may do what it wishes with science— it may interpret its own evidence any way it wishes—but science cannot become the ultimate judge of biblical interpretation or divine revelation.

In that regard I agree with legal scholar Philip Johnson: We must allow "natural science to find its proper place as an important but not all-important part of the life of the mind."[5] For the Christian scholar, science cannot serve as the court of final appeal. None of our disciplines can. For the Christian, the divine revelation of the Holy Scriptures is that bedrock. There is, in fact, a simple reason why science cannot be the ultimate arbiter of truth—science cannot answer the ultimate questions about life.

Recently I was sent a provocative essay that appeared in the January 1997 issue of *First Things*. It was written by Neil Postman, chair of the Department of Culture and Communication at New York University. I read Postman back in 1986 when his stinging critique of television's corrosive effect on American society, *Amusing Ourselves to Death*, was published. His point in this new essay? We have lost the story, the very story that we need. How? He begins with a poem that darkly hints at the how.

> The principal spiritual problem confronting those of us who live in a technological age was spoken of some years ago in a prophetic poem by Edna St. Vincent Millay, in her collection *Huntsman, What Quarry?*

>> Upon this gifted age, in its dark hour,
>> Rains from the sky a meteoric shower
>> Of facts . . . they lie unquestioned, uncombined.
>> Wisdom enough to leech us of our ill
>> Is daily spun, but there exists no loom
>> To weave it into fabric.[6]

Postman seizes her metaphor and cries out, The post-twentieth century information glut that has buried us is killing us because we have "no loom to weave it into fabric." We have lost the stories that could help us or save us from the deluge. How did this come about? Postman goes on to suggest that it resulted from our loss of belief in God.

> It has not been a good pair of centuries for gods. Charles Darwin, we might say, began the great assault by arguing that we were not the children of God, with a capital "G," but of monkeys. His revelation took its toll on him; he suffered from unre-

lieved stomach and bowel pains for which medical historians have failed to uncover a physical cause. Nonetheless, Darwin was unrepentant and hoped that many people would find inspiration, solace, and continuity in the great narrative of evolution. But not many have, and the psychic trauma he induced continues barely concealed to our own day. Karl Marx, who invited Darwin to write an introduction to Das Kapital (Darwin declined), tore to shreds the god of nationalism, showing, with theory and countless examples, how the working classes are deluded into identifying with their capitalist tormentors. Sigmund Freud, working quietly in his consulting room in Vienna, bid to become the world's most ferocious godbuster. He showed that the great god of Reason, whose authority had been certified by the Age of Enlightenment, was a great impostor, that it served mostly to both rationalize and conceal the commands of our most primitive urgings. The cortex [of the brain], as it were, is merely the servant of genitalia. For good measure, Freud destroyed the story of childhood innocence, tried to prove that Moses was not a Jew, and argued that our belief in deities was a childish and neurotic illusion. . . .

The odd thing is that though they differed in temperament, each of these men intended to provide us with a firmer and more humane basis for our beliefs. And some day that may yet happen. Meanwhile, humanity reels from what has been lost. God is dead, Nietzsche said before he went insane. He may have meant gods are dead. If he did, he was wrong. In this century, new gods have rushed in to replace the old but most have had no staying power.[7]

Can science save us? Is science the god who can help us? Postman answers:

> But in the end, science does not provide the answers most of us require. Its story of our origins and of our end is, to say the least, unsatisfactory. To the question, "How did it all begin?" science answers, "Probably by an accident." To the question, "How will it all end?" science answers, "Probably by an accident." And to many people, the accidental life is not worth living. Moreover, the science-god has no answer to the question, "Why are we here?" and, to the question, "What moral instructions do you give us?", the science-god maintains silence. It places itself at the service of both the beneficent and the cruel, and its grand moral impartiality, if not indifference, makes it, in the end, no god at all.[8]

Postman is most certainly right! The story of our origins and creation has been obliterated from our thinking and living. We have lost our story! Somebody has systematically been destroying our story. Now who could that be?

I wish to end with a tale of two stories. Once upon a time in the middle of the nineteenth century, two competing stories were catapulted onto the stage of human awareness. Two stories destined to become locked in a desperate global showdown to the very end of human time.

The first story was birthed in the year 1844—when it began its mission to every nation, kindred, tongue, and people. In the dark twist of unlikely coincidence, the second story was also birthed in the year 1844—July, as a matter of fact, when 189 pages of a manuscript were written out longhand. But the world would not know of that birthing until the story was published in 1859. Not to be outdone, it, too, began its mission to every nation, kindred, tongue, and people. Knowing what is now known, it can hardly be mere coincidence that the two stories would be birthed at the same moment in history and compete for the same global allegiance. Someone, somewhere, was ready and waiting.

What are the two stories? The first story still cries out the words of that lone angel streaking across the midnight heavens of the Apocalypse with his piercing shout at the end of human time: " 'Fear God, and give him glory, for the hour of his judgment has come; and worship him who made heaven and earth, the sea and the springs of water' " (Revelation 14:7). An urgent call to the human race that must be heard: It is the judgment hour—worship your Creator and remember His memorial of Creation, the seventh-day Sabbath, to keep it holy. This is the message that was given with new fervor by the Adventists of the nineteenth century and that remains at the core of Seventh-day Adventism to this day.

Not to be outdone, the second story also cries out into the midnight heavens. Only this story is the dark antithesis, the shadowy opposite of the first story, for the second story now proclaims a bold and strident challenge: There is no creator god to worship, for you are all the god you will ever need. Worship yourself and forget the myth of a creation and the tale of a judgment. This second story is Darwin's tale and is proclaimed with great fervor by evolutionists around the world.

Two stories, birthed at the same mid-century mark once upon a time, and now destined to be locked—these two stories—in a life-and-death struggle for human allegiance until the end of all time. Two stories with two very opposite beginnings and, tragically, two very opposite endings. Two stories: the first story proclaimed by Adventism, the second story propagated by Darwinism. The first a Christian message of hope, the second a godless message of hopelessness.

It is not a choice between religion and science. Not at all! It is in the end the choice between two worldviews, two cosmic stories, two competing kingdoms.

And at the head of one of them stands Jesus Christ who still declares "'The Sabbath was made for humankind, and . . . the Son of Man is lord even of the Sabbath'" (Mark 2:27, 28).

Lord of the Sabbath, Lord of the story. Ladies and gentlemen of the jury, the evidence is not only admissible, it is compelling. The Creator rests His case in your hands.

Why not experience this rest on this Day of Rest for the rest of your life? After all, that's why He gave us the seventh-day Sabbath "in the beginning."

---

1. Anthony F. Aveni, *Empires of Time* (New York: Basic Books Publishers, 1989), 53, 57.

2. Ibid., 87.

3. Ibid., 100, 101.

4. Jacques B. Doukhan, in *The Sabbath in Jewish and Christian Traditions* Tamard C. Eskenazi, Daniel T. Harrington, and William H. Shea eds. (New York: The Crossroad Publishing, 1991), 151.

5. Phillip E. Johnson, *Darwin on Trial* (Downers Grove: InterVarsity Press, 1993), 169.

6. Neil Postman, "Science and the Story That We Need," *First Things*, January 1997, 29.

7. Ibid., 30.

8. Ibid., 31.

CHAPTER EIGHT

Was
John Lennon
Right?

As we come to the end of our journey together, I will be the first to admit that I have not been any better than Albert Einstein's chauffeur.

Perhaps you have heard the story. I have heard it twice, so it surely must be true! Einstein had dyslexia and apparently did not have a driver's license. He was dependent on a chauffeur to drive him from the Princeton campus, where he taught, to various locations for evening lectures—so the story goes. The chauffeur had sat through all those lectures and was quite bored by the thought of doing it again one particular evening. So the driver, in a moment of braggadocio, told the great scientist, as he was driving him to the lecture, that he had memorized his lecture on the theory of relativity and could in fact deliver the entire talk himself. Einstein was tired but bemused and instantly seized the moment and challenged the chauffeur. "OK, tonight you go in as me and I'll go in as you. Nobody knows me here so let's see if you can do it!"

And so the chauffeur was the one who mounted the

platform after the introduction and commenced to deliver the memorized, verbatim lecture on the theory of
relativity. Even Einstein was impressed! At the end, after
the audience applause, before the chauffeur could exit
the platform, the emcee jumped up and asked if there
were any questions to ask of Dr. Einstein. The chauffeur
blanched, but maintained his assumed poise.

Someone in the audience stood up and asked a most
complicated question about the technical ramifications
of Einstein's theory. Scrambling for something—anything—to say, the chauffeur suddenly brightened up:
"Why, my friend, that question is so easy I'm almost in-
sulted. In fact, to show you how elementary your question is, I'm going to ask my chauffeur to come up here
and answer it instead!"

Today I will readily confess that I am no better than
Einstein's chauffeur because, while I have done much
reading and studying on this topic, I cannot answer many
of the questions!

In all candor I must say that it has been a privilege to
share with you my own search for answers—answers that
help to intelligently express and defend faith in the Scriptures in the face of skeptical challenges. I feel strongly
about the issues that I have shared in the previous seven
chapters. As a result of my study in the area of Creation
and Evolution, my own convictions about the strength
and validity of the historical biblical account of Creation
have grown stronger.

You have surely surmised by now that I firmly believe in the logical, internal consistency of the Bible
record and that the great corpus of divine truth in this
human-divine document is bound up with the Creation
account. As I stated, I believe the truth about Creation,
and a Creator God lies at the heart of all other revealed

truth. Yes, I strongly believe in all that we have shared over this journey. Hopefully, along the way, you may have come to the realization that we do not have to be country bumpkins to believe in the historical Genesis account of Creation and the Flood. We can believe in the intelligent integrity of this Book and in God's intention that we be something far more than mere animal products of evolution! We are not destined to come on the scene by accident and to leave the same way. We are humans, created in the image of God. Created to live—to last—forever. We were built to last!

However, as a pastor I must make this point. While you are not a country bumpkin to believe, neither are you a hell-bound infidel if you wrestle with convictions different than those I have expressed here. God makes a beautiful invitation in Isaiah when he cries out, "Come now, and let us reason together" (Isa. 1:18, KJV).

There are two key words in that divine appeal: *Reason*—that's what God invites all His children to do, to exercise all our God-given intellect to examine the data and the Scriptures in order to more deeply understand the true, divinely intended coherence between the Bible and science. *Together*—as Christians, as part of a community of faith and with love for each other and trust in the Lord of Scripture and the Lord of science, we must reason and dialogue and study and journey together.

I paid a late-night visit to a scientist friend of mine in his office. And while our understanding of the biblical account differs and while I have concerns regarding some of his biblical interpretations, our commitment to respect each other must remain constant and unchanged. Both of us must always and ever find in Christ the unfailing source of truth. Jesus said, " 'I am the way, and the truth, and the life' " (John 14:6). I want to call all Christian thinkers to the primacy of the Word of God in all our scholarship and intellectual endeavors. I would not be faithful as a pastor if I did not do so.

One writer once quipped, "God is smarter than I am!" And of course, he's right! Rev. Joan Brown Campbell, speaking at the memorial service in New York for the late great astronomer and author Carl Sagan (an avowed atheist), said: "He would say to me, 'you are so smart; why do you believe in God?' And I'd say, 'You are so smart; why don't you believe in God?' "[1]

The fact is that God is smarter than all of us! Hence, we must begin and end within the covers of the Holy Scriptures, where the Eternal One has called us to meet with Him. Do we reject all other extrabiblical knowledge? Of course not! But where contradictions appear, it is possible that a patient waiting and an earnest, prayerful seeking can resolve apparent tensions between present science and present faith.

Will we resolve all of the issues? Surely not! 1 Corinthians 13:12 is still true. "Now we see in a mirror, dimly, but then we will see face-to-face. Now I know only in part; then I will know fully, even as I have been fully known."

Ancient mirrors were polished pieces of metal and became blurred and bent with use. They were better than nothing but hardly an accurate reflection of reality! The Greek word for "dimly" is *ainigmati,* from whence comes our word, *enigmatic,* a riddle. Someday we will see it all as clearly as being face-to-face—no mirror in between! One day there will be another Creation, and then we shall know the truth at last about the first Creation.

I want to be very blunt with you as we move this book to a close. Can we turn this hell-hole—this fallen, corrupted, dysfunctional planet we call home—into heaven?

John Lennon hoped so before he died in a pool of his own blood on a New York sidewalk. Months before he was tragically gunned down, Lennon wrote, composed, and sang what became his most popular solo work. In it he asks us to imagine that there is no heaven or hell and that people "living for today" will not kill each other over nationalistic or religious differences. In his imaginary world there are no possessions but all behave as brothers, sharing everything. And with these troublesome things set aside, he imagined that the world would be united as one happy, heavenly place.

If only Lennon could have known that the very heaven on earth he dreamed of had already been promised long, long ago!

"I am about to create new heavens and a new earth; the former things shall not be remembered or come to mind" (Isa. 65:17). That's what John Lennon wished for so wistfully—a new world where the old ways are gone forever! How did Lennon put it? "Imagine all the people living life in peace . . ." A new world where the old ways are gone forever! And how does the verse end? "The former things shall not be remembered."

I was studying the Bible with a man who wanted to be baptized. When he read this verse, he asked why God was going to blank out our memories. "Isn't that awfully arbitrary of God—to erase our earthling memories so that the past is wiped out?" Actually, Isaiah is employing a figure of speech that is used a few pages later in Jeremiah 3:16, where the prophet writes, "It shall not come to mind, or be remembered, or missed."

When God creates a new heaven and a new earth with its new society, nobody is going to sit around singing the exact opposite of Lennon's wish: "Imagine there is cancer . . . it's easy if you try . . . imagine there are murders and rapes and robberies on the sly . . . imagine there's more killing, wars, and morgues and courts . . . O, you may say I'm a dreamer, but I'm not the only one. "

Mark it down—there will be no longing, no wistful wishing, for the hell-hole that earth has turned out to be, thanks to Lucifer's rebellion against God. Nobody in that newly recreated earth will ever wish to go back to the former things, so utterly and thoroughly satisfied we will be with God's new creation!

By the way, did you know that there is a guarantee of this new creation tucked away in the original Hebrew of Isaiah 65:17? The Hebrew language in this verse is identical with one other Hebrew verse in the Bible. Can you guess which one? Genesis 1:1—"created . . . heavens . . . earth." Do you know what that means? *The promise of a heaven in the future is based upon the premise of a Creation in the past.*

I went through and examined the major passages describing the new earth in the Old and New Testaments and discovered that the language of a new creation is heavily laced with the language and symbols of the old creation! *The promise of a heaven in the future is based upon the premise of a creation in the past.* If there were no creation in the past, then there would be no heaven in the future. Because, throughout Scripture, the God of the first creation is the God of the last creation. The premise of the former creation is in itself the promise of the future creation. The future is premised on the former. The God who created this world originally has promised to re-create it all over again! Imagine that! This world was built to last, and we are intended to live with God for eternity!

In that intriguing light, permit me now, for the last time (I promise!), to raise the issue we have confronted all along: Since He is the same God, the One who performed the creation in the beginning and the one who will perform it in the end, can we not be certain that His *modus operandus*, his method of creation, will be the same for both creations? Which being interpreted means: However He will re-create the earth in the future, it will surely mirror His method of creating the earth in one week in the past. Does it not seem natural and logical to conclude that God's methods of creation at the beginning and at the end would in fact be the same method? Which again being interpreted means that *if* He chose long ages of gradual natural selection for his Creation in the beginning (as Christian evolutionists suggest), why would He not choose that same method of re-creation in the end?

Anybody who carefully reads Revelation 20 and 21 knows that God's re-creation of a new heaven and a new earth follows immediately upon the heels of a global, cleansing, purifying lake of fire that dissolves the very elements of air and earth in their searing, cleansing flame. There is no eternal hell found in Revelation. Instead, this earth is consumed and cleansed by flames. And when the fires are finished, the very next words of the Apocalypse borrow Isaiah's promise of God's creation of a new heaven and a new earth. "Then I saw a new heaven and a new earth; for the first heaven and the first earth had passed away, and the sea was no more" (Rev. 21:1).

Will He take millions of years to do it then? No! Almost every Bible scholar would agree. He will re-create it by (here is their technical term for it) *ex nihilo divine fiat Creation*: From out of nothing by His word He will create a new heavens and a new earth! He won't take billions of years to create a new heaven and a new earth! He can't. The New Jerusalem will be situated on this now molten hunk of rock, awaiting the promise of a new creation! And if He does it quickly at the end, isn't it utterly consistent to conclude that Genesis was absolutely right in describing Him as doing it that way "in the beginning"? *Ex nihilo divine fiat Creation.*

When we witness that new creation with our own eyes—and by God's grace you and I are going to be there—then seeing will be believing, and believing will be seeing! At last we will see it. For now we must look through a mirror dimly, but then it shall be face-to-face!

> I am about to create new heavens
>> and a new earth;
>> the former things shall *not* be
>>> remembered or come to mind.
>> But be glad and rejoice forever
>>> in what I am creating;
>> for I am about to create Jerusalem as a joy,
>>> and its people as a delight.
> I will rejoice in Jerusalem,
>> and delight in my people;
> *no* more shall the sound of weeping
>> be heard in it, or the cry of distress.
> *No* more shall there be in it an infant
>> that lives but a few days,
> or an old person who does not
>> live out a lifetime;
> for one who dies at a hundred years
>> will be considered a youth,
> and one who falls short of a hundred
>> will be considered accursed.
> They shall build houses and inhabit them;
>> they shall plant vineyards and eat
>> their fruit.
> They shall *not* build and another inhabit;

they shall *not* plant and another eat;
for like the days of a tree shall the
    days of my people be,
and my chosen shall long enjoy
    the work of their hands.
They shall *not* labor in vain,
    or bear children for calamity;
for they shall be offspring blessed by the Lord—
    and their descendants as well (Isa.
    65:17-23).

I heard a loud voice from
    the throne saying,
" 'See, the home of God is among mortals.
    He will dwell with them as their God;
they will be his peoples, and
    God himself will be with them;
he will wipe every tear from their eyes.
    Death will be *no* more;
mourning and crying and pain will be *no* more,
    for the first things have passed away' "
    (Rev. 21:3, 4).

Did you notice the repetition of the words *no* and *not?* It's an astounding thought, but both Isaiah and John the revelator use the same tactic. They keep accessing that single negative prohibition to describe the new earth. No, No, No! No more death (we have all traveled in too many funeral corteges), no more tears (tears from courtrooms to county hospitals to cemeteries), no more dying (not even dying with dignity, if that is possible), no more pain, no more hurt, no more destruction.

The very same word *no* John Lennon kept repeating over and over in his wistful wish for a new world without heaven. Oh, John, if only you had known that the heaven you didn't want is the new world that will turn out to be what you wanted most of all. "Imagine there's no heaven. " Oh no! Imagine there *is* a heaven, a new heaven and a new earth. Where all the Nos nobody wants will never be there again! So radically different is God's newly created earth from this fallen earth we call home that the writers who caught a vision of it could only find adequate language by saying **No, No, No.**

Harry Blamires has put it this way in an essay:

> If only we could have the positives of earthly life without the negatives. But that is precisely what heaven has to offer—the removal of the negatives. . . . [In heaven] both [human sin and the dominion of time] will be swept away. Here below, time withers flowers and human beauty, it encourages good intentions to evaporate, it deprives us of our loved ones. Within the universe ruled by time, the happiest marriage ends in death, the loveliest woman becomes a skeleton. Fading and aging, losing and failing, being deprived and being frustrated—these are the negative aspects of life in time. Life in eternity will liberate us from all loss, all deprivation.[2]

"Imagine all the people living life in peace. You may say I'm a dreamer, but I'm not the only one. I hope someday you'll join us, and the world will live as one."

Oh, my friend, I want to be there, don't you? What John Lennon imagined, the Bible has promised. No more tears, no more pain, no more death, no more hospitals, no more divorce courts, no more jail houses, no more tenements, no more hunger, no more guilt, no more sin!

Where all the Nos nobody wants will never be there again! No more of all the Nos we know more about than we ever wanted to know!

I want to be there, but not because of all the Nos. I want to be there because of the *Yes*. For *Yes*, my Creator will be there—and that is why I must be there too. And when one day I hold His nail-scarred hands in mine and, through tears of joy, gaze down upon those purple scars that shall never be re-created away, then I will know that my Creator has always said *Yes* for me! Once, when He said *Yes* and made me. Twice, when He said *Yes* and saved me. Thrice, when He said *Yes* and brought me home at last. *Yes, Yes, Yes*.

With a *YES* like that, how could anyone say *NO* to the Creator?

---

1. I wish to thank Paul Hamel for bringing this quotation to my attention.

2. Harry Blamires, "The Eternal Weight of Glory," *Christianity Today*, May 27, 1991, 30.